C000050619

ABERDEEN
CITY ATLAS

Contents

Key to Street Map Symbols	2
Key to Street Map Pages	3
City Centre Map	4-5
Street Maps	6-41
Local Information	42-43
Places of Interest	44-47
Key to Road Map Symbols	48
Key to Road Map Pages	49
Road Maps	50-55
Index to Street Names	56-69
Index to Place Names	70-72

Published by Collins
An imprint of HarperCollins*Publishers*
77-85 Fulham Palace Road, Hammersmith, London W6 8JB

HarperCollins website : www.**fire**and**water**.com
Bartholomew website : www.bartholomewmaps.com
e-mail: roadcheck@harpercollins.co.uk

Copyright © HarperCollins*Publishers* Ltd 2001
Mapping © Bartholomew Ltd 2001

Mapping generated from Bartholomew digital databases

Printed in Hong Kong   ISBN 0 00 711219 X   NI10750 CCDD

HarperCollins*Publishers*

② Key to Street Map Symbols

A74	Primary road dual/single
A89	A Road dual/single
B763	B Road dual/single
	Other road dual/single
	Road under construction
Toll → I	One-way street/Toll

	Restricted access street
	Pedestrian street
	Minor road/Track
FB	Footpath/Footbridge
	Unitary authority boundary
	Postcode boundary

	Railway line
⤬ ⊢ ⊢	Level crossing/Railway tunnel
⇌ ⇌	Main/Other railway station
⬤	Bus/Coach station

P+🚌	Park & Ride
P	Car Park
— — — —	Vehicle Ferry
- - - - - -	Pedestrian Ferry

	Leisure/Tourism		Education
🎥	Multiplex cinema		Health
	Shopping/Retail		Industry/Commerce
	Administration/Law		Notable building

Pol	Police station	✚	Major religious building
PO	Post Office	+ ☾ ✡	Church/Mosque/Synagogue
		🎥	Cinema
Lib	Library	🎭	Theatre
■	Fire station/Ambulance station/Community centre	i i	Tourist information centre (all year/seasonal)

	Wood/Forest	⚑	Golf course
	Park/Garden/Recreation ground	† † † †	Cemetery
	Public open space		Built up area

15	National Grid number	**15**▶	Page continuation number

SCALE: 4 inches to 1 mile (6.3 cm to 1 km)

0	1/4	1/2	3/4	1 mile

| 0 | 1/4 | 1/2 | 3/4 | 1 | 1 1/4 | 1 1/2 kilometres |

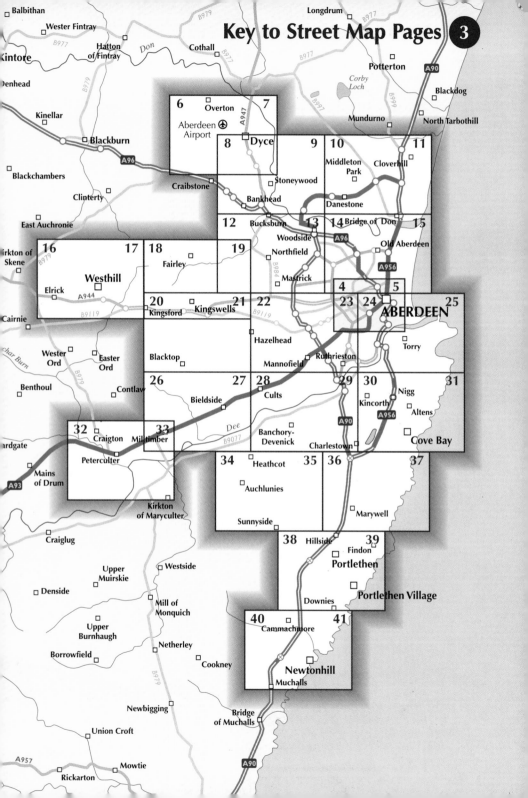

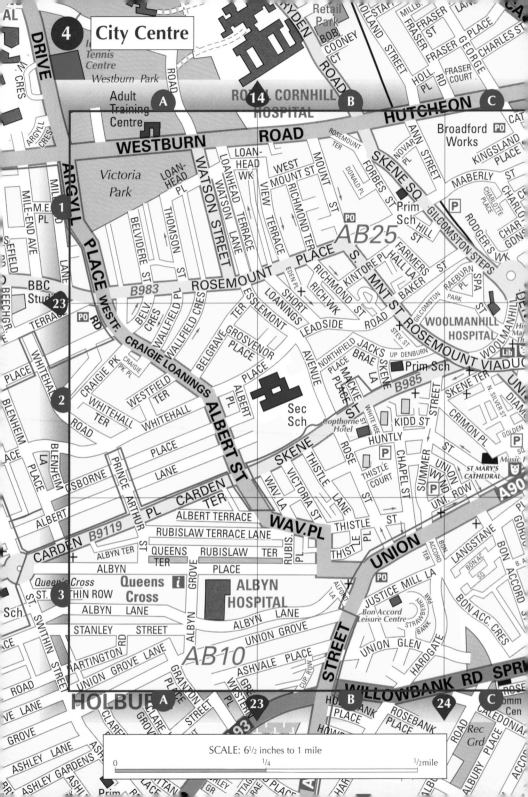

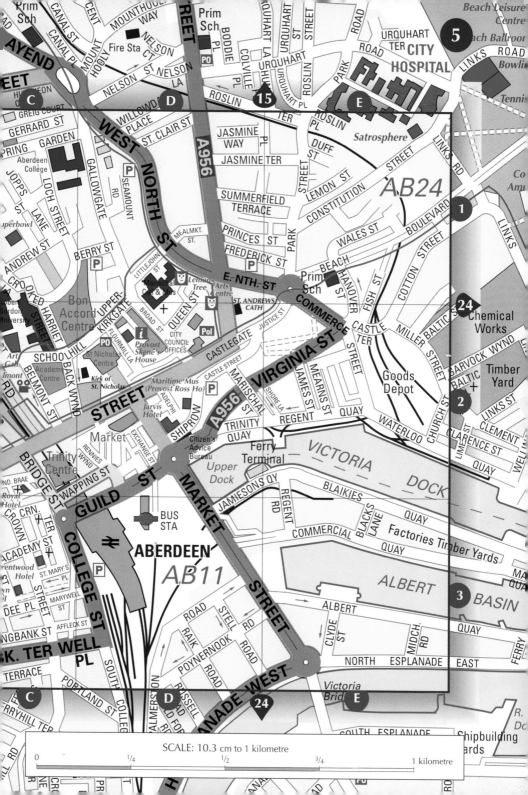

SCALE: 10.3 cm to 1 kilometre

0   1/4   1/2   3/4   1 kilometre

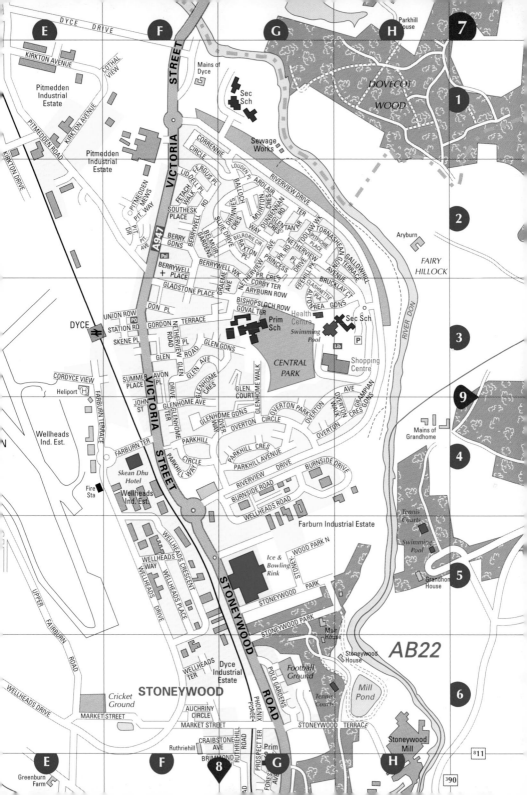

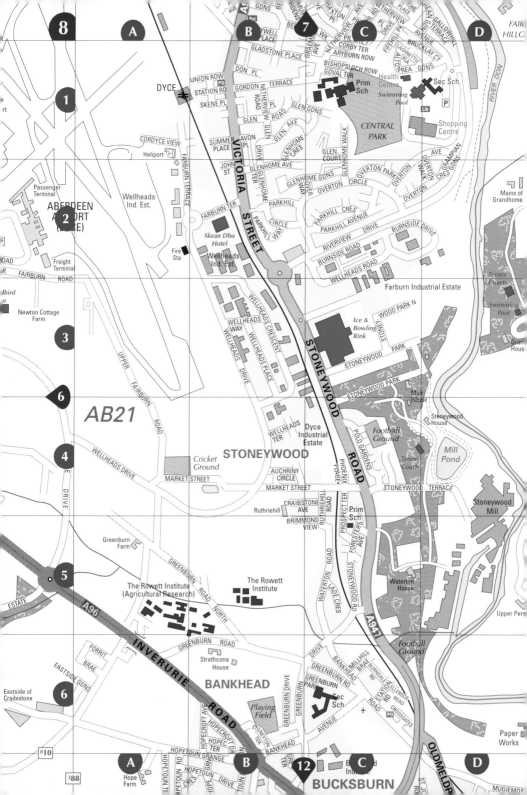

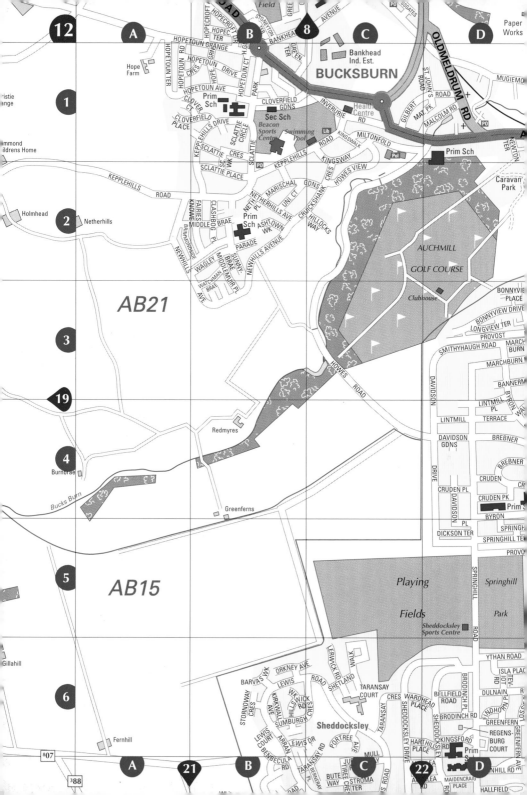

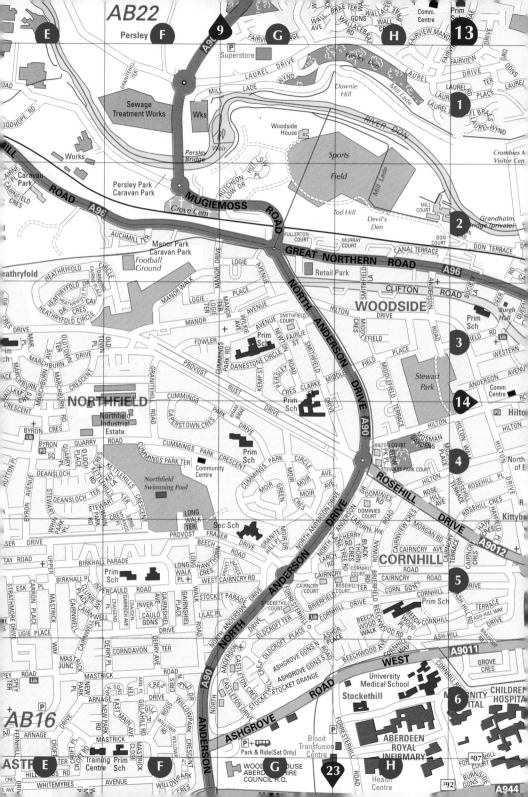

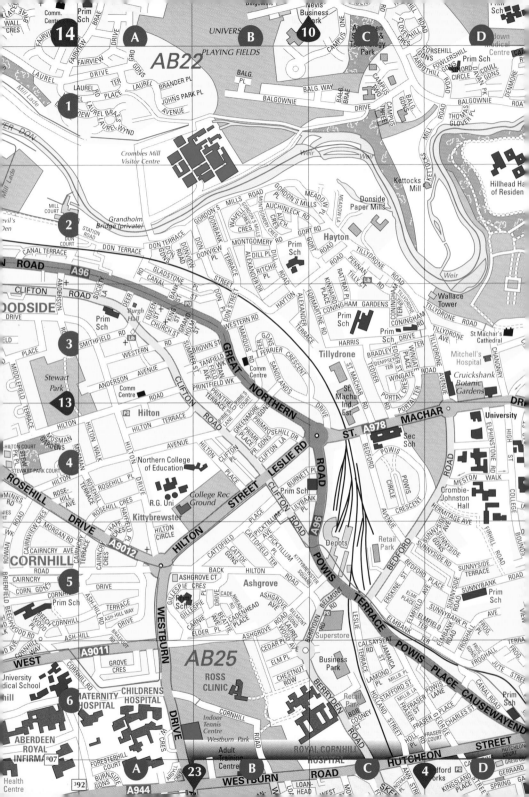

E F G H **17**

1

2

P

Easter
Mains

Borrowstone

3

WESTHILL

18

Longcairn

AB15

4

COURTS
WAY
ANDS DRIVE
CLOSE
CRESCENT
DRIVE
CRESCENT
HILLVIEW ROAD
HILLVIEW AVE
GULLYMOSS VIEW
HILLSIDE VIEW
GULLYMOSS CRES
GULLYMOSS GDNS
CRAIGSTON GDNS
RDENS
HILLSIDE
HILLSIDE
HILLSIDE
GULLYMOSS PLACE
GULLYMOSS
ROAD
CRAIGSTON RD
CRAIGSTON PLACE
HILLSIDE
EASTSIDE DRIVE
EASTSIDE GRN
CRAIGSTON GRN
CRAIGSTON PLACE
MAINS VIEW
SOUTER CIRCLE
BR CRES
MAINS DRIVE
SOUTER GDNS
BRAECROFT DR
BRAE. AVE.
EASTSIDE AVE
MAINS GDNS
MAINS CIRCLE
Mains of
Kinmundy
WAY
Prim
Sch
KINMUNDY GREEN
WYNFORD LA
MAINS DRIVE
BARRIAGER LA
Swimming
Pool
Hall
KINMUNDY GDNS
KINMUNDY
MAINS CT
WRIGHT WALK
TRINITY CT
KINMUNDY AVE
DRIVE
BRODIACH
GORDON GDNS
ASH CT
KIRK CT
KINMUNDY
DEAN GDNS
BRODIACH CT
WESTHILL
ROAD
SHDALE
GRANT CL
Pol
Westhill
Shopping
Centre PO
Brodiach
Tennis Courts
Bowling
Denman Park
ARNHALL DRIVE
ARNHALL CRES
LAWSONDALE DR
LAWSONDALE CRES
LAWSONDALE TER
Cairdhillock
*Arnhall Moss
Nature Reserve*
LAWSON
AVE
5

D

Arnhall
Business
Park

Kingsfo

6

East Fiddie

Mains of
Fiddie

B9119

Bishopsdams

Backhill

⁸06

E F G H

³85

AB21

Map grid references (top): E · F · G · H · 12 · 19

Map grid references (bottom): E · F · G · H

Grid markers (right side): 1 · 2 · 3 · 12 · 4 · 5 · 6

Overhills

NEW
BAGLEY
BRAE
MIDDLEMUIR PL
WATCHMAN
BRAE
SUN
HILLS AVENUE
PARADE

HOWES
ROAD

Redmyres

Burnbrae

Bucks Burn

Greenferns

LS CRESCENT
CONCRAIG
PL
CONCRAIG
GDNS
WELLSIDE RD
WELLSIDE WALK
WELLSIDE
WYND
WELLSIDE CIRCLE
WELLSIDE PL
CRESCENT
IDE AVE
WELLSIDE PARK
IDE PL
ILSIDE PL
WELLSIDE
END

ELLS

Gillahill

Fernhill

Newpark

ORKNEY AVE
BARVAS WK
LEWIS
WICK
ROAD
SHETLAND
LERWICK RD
WALK
TARAN
COURT
STORNOWAY CRES
KIRKWALL
AVE
HILLSWICK
RD
SUMBURGH CRES
LEWIS
GARDENS
4
Sheddocksley
LEWIS
COURT
ARRAN
PL
LEWIS DR
PORTREE AVE
BENBECULA RD
JURA
PL
TIREE CRES
MUL
TAKANSAY RD
HERNIAN PL
BUTE
WAY
STROMA
TER
UIST ROAD
AVE
COLONSAY
CRES
Whitemyres
SCALPAY WALK
PAT
WALK
COLL
WALK
BARRA WK
ERISKAY RD
RAASAY
GDNS
5

LANG STRACHT

LANG
STRACHT
Whitemyres
Holdings
FARA CL
CAVA CL
BRESSAY BRAE
SAMPHREY RD
Tennis
Courts

LANG
East
xterstone
A944
Maidencraig
Den Bu

Gateside
B9119
SKENE
MAIDENC
WOO
ROAD
6
QUEENS DE

JOHN ARTHUR CT
OLD SKENE ROAD
Smithfield

Bellfield
Jess
Pigg
Swimm
Pool
06
GR DA

21
Hazlehead
389

E **F** **19** **G** **H** **21** Sheddocksley

Fern

Newpark

Whitemyres

1

LANG STRACHT

STRACHT

LANG

East xterstone

Whitemyres Holdings

FARA CL CAVA CL

BRESSAY BRAE

SAMPHREY RD

A944

Maidencraig

Tennis Courts

Gateside

B9119 SKENE ROAD

MAIDENCE WOOD

2

QUEENS RD

JOHN ARTHUR CT

OLD SKENE ROAD

Smithfield

Bellfield

Jessiefield Piggery

Swimming Pool

GROATS

AB15

Hazlehead Crematorium

Sec Sch

3

Maryfield

P

Clubhouse

22 Pitch & Putt

Car Pa

HAZLEHEAD

Piper Alpha Memorial

GOLF COURSE

4 HAZLEH

of swells

Wardhead

Haz Nur

5

DEN

WOOD

Loanhead

Mains of Countesswells

ells

6

ntesswells House

Mains of Hillhead

Colthill

27

Thornhill

CRAIGTON ROAD

E **F** **G** **H**

B04

389 Waldorf

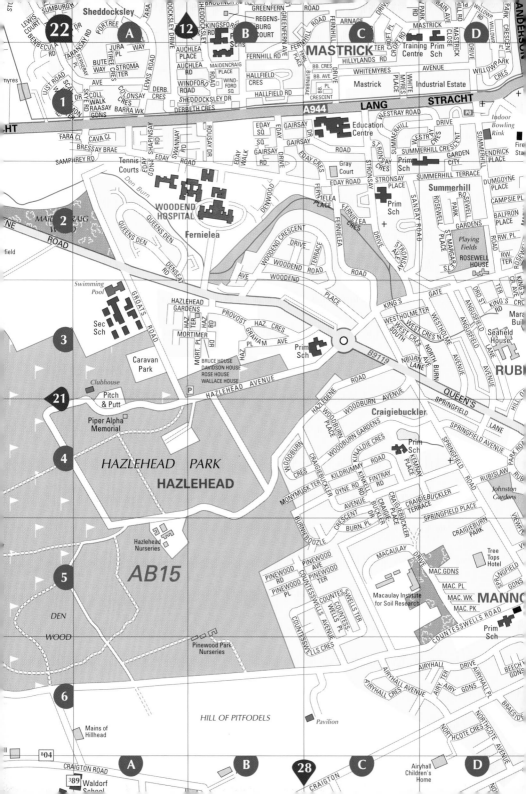

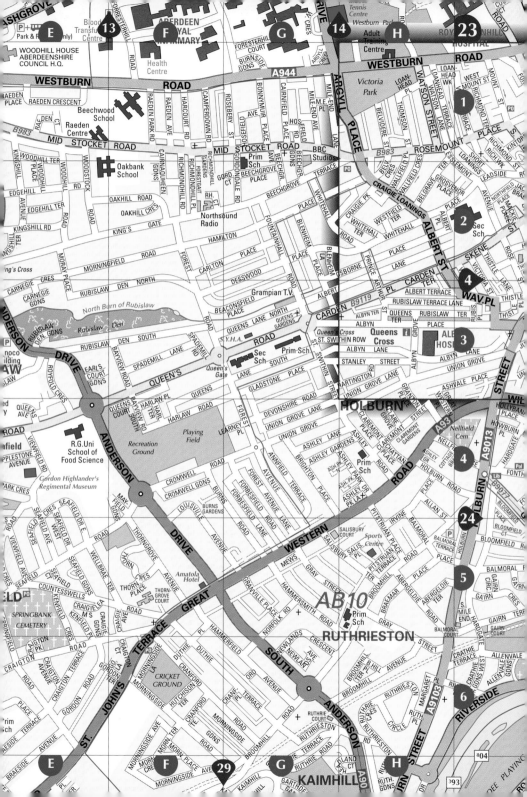

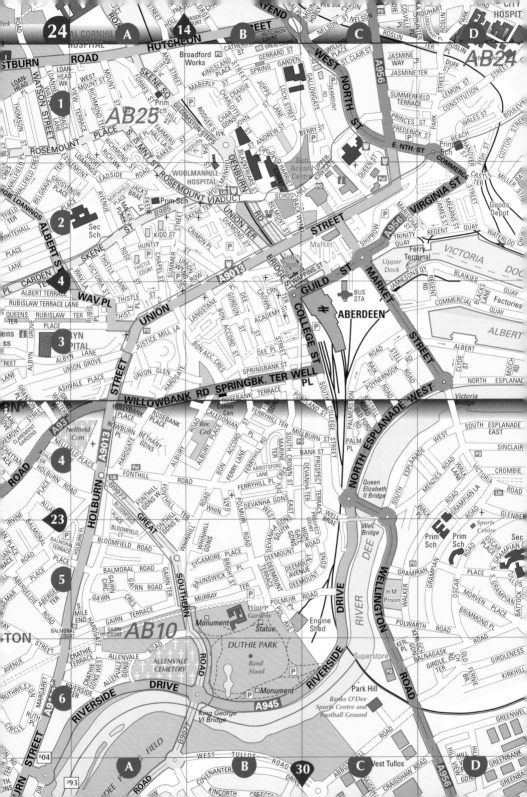

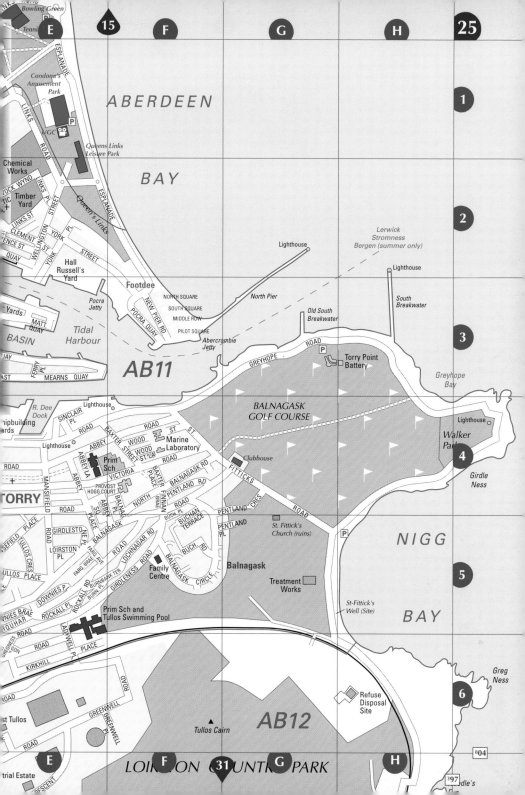

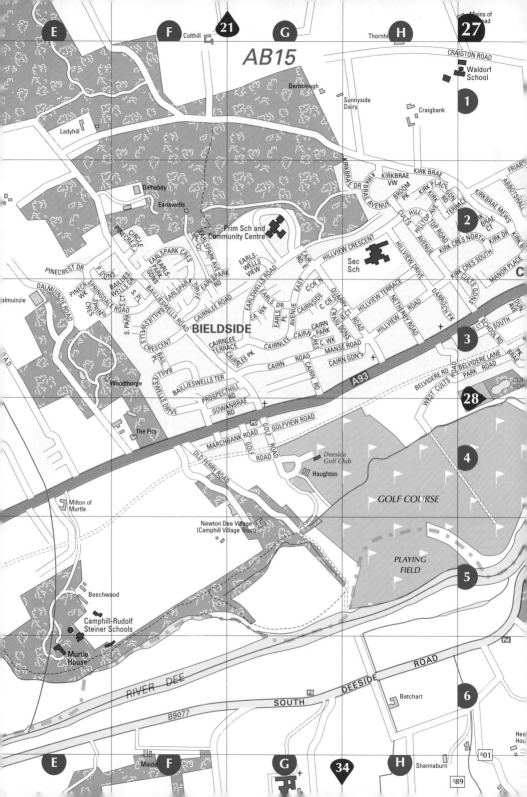

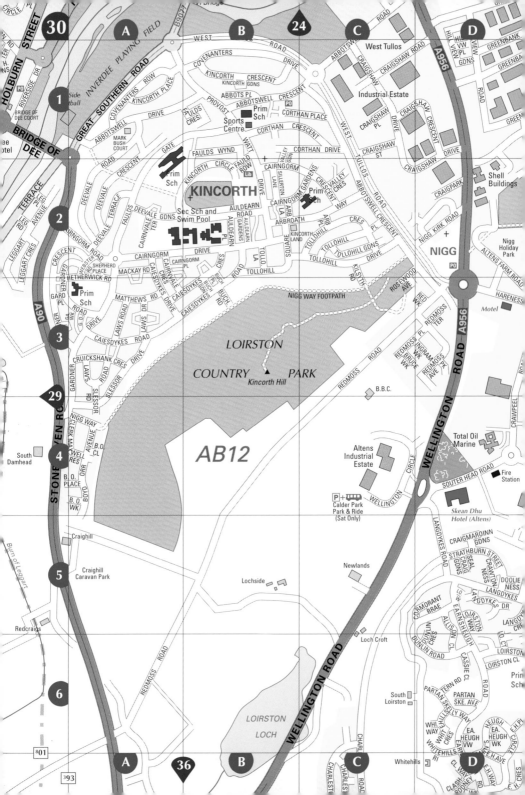

st Tullos

GREENWELL PL

GREENWELL ROAD

ROAD

CRESCENT

strial Estate

Tullos Cairn ▲

LOIRSTON COUNTRY PARK

Needle's Eye

1

Baron's Cairn ▲

Crab's Cairn ▲

Doonies Yawns

Peterseat

Doonies Model Farm

Cat Cairn ▲

Adam's Pots

2

MINTO AVENUE

MINTO AVENUE

MINTO DRIVE

MINTO DRIVE

North Broad Craig

MINTO ROAD

ALTENS

Aberdeen College

Long Slough Cave of Red Rocks

Robin Hood Yawns

3

MINTO ROAD

CIRCLE

HARENESS PK

HARENESS

Hasman Rocks

Altens Haven

BLACKNESS ROAD

Altens Industrial Estate

BLACKNESS AVE

Seals Hole

4

SOUTER HEAD ROAD

Burnbanks

P

Burnbanks Haven

Souter Head

5

MARCHMOUNT ST

SKELLY ROCK

SCURDIE NESS

MARCHM PL

SHINDON NESS

ANNAT BANK

TODD

SHIELDHILL GDNS

MARCHMONT

RICHMOUSAY ST

NESS

GDNS

LOIR

Bunstane Cove

MANOR

Well Cove

Black Cove

Cove Rangers F.C.

FALKLAND AVE

LOIRSTON

The Poor Man

CATTO CRES

SIN. PL

CLAIR CRES

SIN PL

LOIRSTON ROAD

The Graves

PINE WOOD PL

SIN. TER

NBUTTS CRES

REDWOOD CRES

COLSEA TER

COVE BAY

Crawpeel Shore

The Graves

Whitehills

Crawpeel Shore

Long Craig

Prim Sch

Cove Road

Harbour
Cove Shore

The Priest

The Kettle

Hare Ness

South
Blackhill

Horse Shoe

Blackhills
of Cairnrobin

Bareside Point

Blowup Nose

Red Mantle

Earnsheugh Bay

1

2

3

4

5

6

Moss-side

1

FINDON ROAD
FINDON PL
FINDON
Findon Farm
EARNSH.
EA. TER
OLD INN ROAD
RD

Mains of
Findon

THISTLE DRIVE
BARCLAYHILL PLACE
DRIVE
THISTLE
NINIAN PLACE
PIPER PL
CLAYMORE AVE
VIKING PL
ARGYLL PLACE
COOKSTON ROAD
DEVENICK DRIVE

2

Mill of
Findon

Findon Shore

Mains of
Portlethen

May Craig

3

GLEBE
COURT
HILLSIDE TER
BURN-
SIDE
GDNS
Prim Sch
COOKSTON ROAD
Lib
Pol
PORTLETHEN
Medical
Centre
THE
SQ
PO
HEATHER PL
BRUNT
MOOR
PORTLETHEN

PORTLETHEN
VILLAGE

4

BROADHAVEN RD
CRAIGMARN
ARN PL
RD
HARLEY
TER
Portlethen
Bay
OLD COAST RD

DOWNIES ROAD

5

D

Portlethen
Bay

Cammachmore
Bay

6

Berrymuir Head

Bay

Mains of
Clashfarquhar

39

DOWNIES

Berrymuir Head

Burn of Daff

Clashfarquhar Bay

Cobleboards

Cran
Hill

Floors Craig

1

2

3

DUNLIN
COURT
PLOVER
COURT
TURNSTONE
COURT
FULMAR
COURT
TERN
COURT
PUFFIN
COURT
SANDERLING
COURT

Craig Stirling

MILL ROAD

NEWT.
CRAN
BRAE
BETTRIDGE RD
SKATERAW RD
HILL
CHAPEL RD
AND.
DR
CRANHILL RD
MURRAY RD
CRAIG PL
PO
VILLA RD
HEAD
SOUTH HEADLANDS CRES

Newtonhill
Bay

Whiteland Head

4

Bowling
Green

May
Craig

5

6

USEFUL INFORMATION

Aberdeen and Grampian Tourist Board, 27 Albyn Place
AB10 1YL *Tel: 01224 632727   Web Site: www.agtb.org*
4 A3

Central Library, Rosemount Viaduct AB25 1GW
Tel: 01224 652500 **4 C2**

Grampian Police, Force Headquarters, Queen Street
AB10 1ZA *Tel: 01224 386000*
Web Site: www.grampian.police.uk **5 D2**

Main Post Offices
St.Nicholas Shopping Centre, St. Nicholas Street
AB10 1HW *Tel: 01224 633081* **5 D2**

489 Union Street AB11 6AZ *Tel: 01224 581041*
Web Site: www.postoffice-counters.co.uk **4 B3**

Tourist Information Centre, St.Nicholas House, Broad Street
AB10 1DE *Tel: 01224 632727* **5 D2**

ADMINISTRATION

Aberdeen City Council
Web Site: www.aberdeencity.gov.uk
St. Nicholas House, Broad Street AB10 1BX
Tel: 01224 522000 **5 D2**

Town House, Broad Street AB10 1AQ
Tel: 01224 522501 **5 D2**

38 Powis Terrace, Kittybrewster AB25 3RF
Tel: 01224 480281 **15 E5**

74-76 Spring Garden AB25 1GN
Tel: 01224 522020 **5 C1**

Summerhill Education Centre, Stronsay Drive
AB15 6JA *Tel: 01224 346060* **22 C1**

Aberdeenshire Council
Web Site: www.aberdeenshire.gov.uk
Woodhill House, Westburn Road
AB16 5GB *Tel: 01224 682222* **23 E1**

ENTERTAINMENT

Cinemas
The Belmont, 49 Belmont Street AB10 1JS
Tel: 01224 343536   Information: 01224 343534
Web Site: www.picturehouse-cinemas.co.uk **5 C2**

UGC Cinemas, Queens Links Leisure Park, Leisure Road
AB11 5BT *Tel: 01224 572228   Information: 0541 550502*
25 E1

Theatres / Concert Halls
Arts Centre, 33 King Street AB24 5AA
Tel: 01224 635208 **5 D1**

Exhibition & Conference Centre, Bridge of Don AB23 8BL
Tel: 01224 824824   Web Site www.aecc.co.uk **11 F5**

His Majesty's Theatre, Rosemount Viaduct AB25 1GL
Tel: 01224 641122 **4 C2**

Lemon Tree, Cafe Theatre, 5 West North Street AB24 5AT
Tel: 01224 642230   Web Site: www.lemontree.org
5 D1

Music Hall, Union Street AB10 1QS
Tel: 01224 641122 **4 C2**

FURTHER EDUCATION

Aberdeen College, Gallowgate Centre, Gallowgate
AB25 1BN *Tel: 01224 612000*
Web Site: www.abcol.ac.uk **5 C1**

Robert Gordon University, Schoolhill AB10 1FR
Tel: 01224 262000   Web Site: www.rgu.ac.uk **5 C2**

Northern College of Education, Aberdeen Campus,
Hilton Place AB24 4FA *Tel: 01224 283500*
Web Site: www.norcol.ac.uk **14 A4**

University of Aberdeen, King's College AB24 3FX
Tel: 01224 273504   Web Site:www.abdn.ac.uk **14 D4**

HEALTH

Grampian University Hospitals NHS Trust
Web Site: www.show.scot.nhs.uk/guh
Aberdeen Royal Infirmary, Foresterhill AB25 2ZN
Tel: 01224 681818   A&E Department **13 H6**

Aberdeen Maternity Hospital, Foresterhill, Cornhill Road
AB25 2Z *Tel : 01224 840606* **14 A6**

Raeden Centre, Midstocket Road AB15 5PD
Tel: 01224 321381 **23 E1**

Royal Aberdeen Children's Hospital, Foresterhill,
Cornhill Road AB25 2ZG *Tel: 01224 681818*
A&E Department **14 A6**

Roxburghe House, Tor-Na-Dee Hospital,
Milltimber AB13 0HR
Tel: 01224 681818 **26 C4**

Tor-Na-Dee Hospital, Milltimber AB13 0HR
Tel: 01224 681818 **26 C4**

Woodend Hospital, Eday Road AB15 6XS
Tel: 01224 663131 **22 B2**

Woolmanhill Hospital, Old Infirmary Buildings,
Woolmanhill AB25 1LD *Tel: 01224 681818* **4 C2**

Grampian Primary Care NHS Trust
Web Site: www.gpct.org.uk
Royal Cornhill Hospital, Cornhill Road
AB25 2ZH *Tel: 01224 663131* **13 H6**

City Hospital, Urquhart Road
AB24 5AU *Tel: 01224 663131* **15 F6**

Woodlands Hospital, Craigton Road, Cults
AB15 9PR *Tel: 01224 663131* **28 B1**

Independent Hospitals
Albyn Hospital, 21-24 Albyn Place AB9 1RJ
Tel: 01224 595993
Web Site: www.ppphealthcare.co.uk **4 A3**

HELP AND ADVICE

Childline *Tel: 0800 1111   Web Site: www.childline.org.uk*

Citizen's Advice Bureau, 47 Market Street AB11 5PZ
Tel: 01224 586255   Web Site:www.nacab.org.uk **5 D2**

Missing Persons *Tel: 0500 700 700*
Web Site: www.missingpersons.org

NSPCC Helpline *Tel: 0808 800500*
Web Site: www.nspcc.org.uk

Rape Crisis Centre, 1-3, Little Belmont Street AB10 1JG
Tel: 01224 620772 Web Site: www.rapecrisis.co.uk

RSPCA *Tel: 0870 444 3127   Web Site: www.rspca.org.uk*

Samaritans, 60 Dee Street AB11 6DS
Tel: 01224 574488
Web Site: www.samaritans.org.uk

Victim Support   *Web Site: www.victimsupport.com*
4 Albyn Place AB10 1YH   *Tel: 01224 622478*
47 Belmont St AB10 1JS   *Tel: 01224 647456*

MEDIA
Local Newpapers
Aberdeen Press & Journal   *Tel: 01224 690222*
Aberdeen & District Independent   *Tel: 01224 618300*
Aberdeen Evening Express   *Tel: 01224 690222*
Aberdeen Herald & Post   *Tel: 01224 631872*

Local Radio
Northsound One FM 96.9, 97.6, 103 MHz
Tel: 01224 337000   Web Site: www.northsound.co.uk

Northsound Two AM 1035 kHz
Tel: 01224 337000   Web Site: www.northsound.co.uk

SPORT & LEISURE
Association Football
Aberdeen Football Club, Pittodrie Stadium, Pittodrie Street
AB24 5QH   *Tel: 01224 632328 Web Site: www.afc.co.uk*
15 F5

Golf
Auchmill Golf Club, Bonnyview Road,
West Heathryfold AB21 9RR   *Tel: 01224 714577* **12 D3**

Balnagask Golf Club, St. Fitticks Road
AB11 9QT   *Tel: 01224 8764* **25 G4**

Deeside Golf Club, Golf Road, Bieldside
AB15 9DL   *Tel: 01224 869457* **27 G4**

Hazlehead Golf Club, Hazlehead
AB15 8BD   *Tel: 01224 321830* **22 A3**

Kings Links Golf Centre, Golf Road
AB24 5QB   *Tel: 01224 632269* **15 F5**

Murcar Golf Club, Bridge of Don
AB23 8BD   *Tel: 01224 704354* **11 H2**

Portlethen Golf Club, Badentoy Road,
Portlethen AB12 4YA   *Tel: 01224 781090* **38 C2**

Royal Aberdeen Golf Club, Links Road,
Bridge of Don AB23 8AT   *Tel: 01224 702571* **15 G1**

Westhill Golf Club, Westhill Heights, Westhill
AB32 6RY   *Tel: 01224 742567* **16 C3**

Shopping
Aberdeen Market, 8-10, Market Street AB11 5NX
Tel: 01224 575576 **5 D2**

Academy Shopping Centre, Schoolhill AB10 1LB
Tel: 01224 633009 **5 C2**

Bon Accord Centre, George Street AB25 1HZ
Tel: 01224 647470 **5 C2**

St. Nicholas Centre, St. Nicholas Street AB10 1HW
Tel: 01224 645420 **5 D2**

Trinity Shopping Centre, Union Street AB11 6BD
Tel: 01224 580076 **5 C2**

Sports/Leisure Centres/Swimming Pools
Banks O'Dee Sports Centre, Abbotswell Road
AB12 3AB   *Tel: 01224 893333* **24 C6**

Beach Leisure Centre, Sea Beach, Esplanade
AB24 5NR   *Tel: 01224 647647* **15 G6**

Beacon Community Educational Centre, Kepplehills Road
AB21 9DG   *Tel: 01224 712889* **12 B1**

Bon Accord Baths & Leisure Centre, Justice Mill Lane
AB11 6EQ   *Tel: 01224 587920* **4 B3**

Bridge of Don Sports Centre, Cardens Knowe,
Scotsdown Road AB22 8RR   *Tel: 01224 826769* **10 D6**

Bucksburn Swimming Pool, Kepplehills Road
AB21 9DG   *Tel: 01224 716479* **12 C1**

Hazlehead Swimming Pool, Groats Road
AB15 8BE   *Tel: 01224 310062* **22 A3**

Kincorth Sports Centre, Corthan Crescent
AB12 5BB   *Tel: 01224 879759* **30 B1**

Kincorth Swimming Pool, Cairngorm Drive
AB12 5NL   *Tel: 01224 872227* **30 B2**

Lynx Ice Arena, Sea Beach, Esplanade
AB24 5NR   *Tel: 01224 649930* **15 G6**

Northfield Swimming Pool, Kettlehills Crescent
AB16 5LR   *Tel: 01224 680307* **13 F4**

Peterculter Sports Centre, Coronation Road, Peterculter
AB14 0RX   *Tel: 01224 732069* **33 E3**

Queens Links Leisure Park, Links Road
AB24 5NL   *Tel: 01224 626755* **25 E1**

Sheddocksley Sports Centre, Springhill Road
AB16 6NZ   *Tel: 01224 692534* **12 D5**

Torry Sports Centre, Oscar Road, Victoria Road
AB11 8ER   *Tel: 01224 871213* **24 D5**

Westburn Sports Centre, Westburn Park,
Westburn Road AB25 2DF   *Tel: 01224 641719* **14 B6**

TRANSPORT
Air
Aberdeen Airport, Dyce AB21 0DU   *Tel: 01224 722331*
Web Site: www.baa.co.uk **6 D4**

Ferry
P&O Scottish Ferries, Jamieson's Quay AB11 5NP
Tel: 01224 589111/572615
Web Site: www.poscottishferries.co.uk **5 D2**

Rail
Railway Station, Guild Street **5 D3**
National Enquiries Tel: 08457 484950
Web Site: www.railtrack.co.uk

Bus
Bus Station, Guild Street AB11 6GR **5 D3**

Bluebird Buses, Guild Street AB11 6GR
Tel: 01224 212266

First Aberdeen, 395 King Street AB9 1SP
Tel: 01224 650000   Information: 01224 650065
Web Site: www.firstaberdeen.co.uk

Park & Ride *Tel: 01224 650000*:
    Exhibition and Conference Centre, Bridge of Don **11 F6**
    Calder Park (Saturday only), Wellington Circle **30 C4**
    Woodhill House (Saturday only), Westburn Road **13 G6**

☐ Indicates a place of interest that appears in the street map pages. An explanation of the other symbols can be found on page 48.

☐ **Aberdeen Art Gallery** 5 C2
The gallery features Scottish, French and 20c English paintings and collections of silver and glass. Spencer, Nash, Bacon and sculptor Henry Moore are among British artists represented.

☐ **Aberdeen Maritime Museum** 5 D2
A museum focusing on fishing, shipbuilding and the offshore oil industry with multi-media displays. Exhibits include a 22 foot (8.5 metre) high model of an oil platform and there is a collection of maritime paintings. The entrance to the 15c Provost Ross's house is through the museum, which is located at Shiprow in Aberdeen.

🏛 **Aberdeenshire Farming Museum** 51 E3
A working farm and museum illustrating regional farming history, in Aden Country Park.

ⓜ **Aberlemno Sculptured Stones** 54 D4
Located in the churchyard at Aberlemno, an upright cross slab (Historic Scotland) with Pictish symbols and combat relief. There are three other stones nearby, beside the B9134.

🎇 **Aden Country Park** 51 E3
A country park covering 230 acres (93 hectares) on the Buchan estate, which dates from the 18c. Features include a wildlife discovery centre, sensory garden, ruined mansion, nature trails and woodland walks. It is also the location of the Aberdeenshire Farming Museum.

🏛 **Angus Folk Museum** 54 B5
Housed in a row of 18c cottages (National Trust for Scotland) in Glamis, the museum has a collection of 19c domestic furniture and memorabilia and also agricultural artefacts.

✚ **Arbroath Abbey** 55 E5
Substantial remains of a Tironensian monastery (Historic Scotland) in the centre of Arbroath. Founded in 1178 by William the Lion, King of Scots, the abbey is linked with Scottish nationalism. The Declaration of Arbroath asserting Scotland's independence from England was signed at the abbey in 1320, and the Stone of Destiny was found here in 1951, having been taken from Westminster Abbey. An abbot's house is among the most notable ruins.

🏛 **Arbuthnot Museum** 51 G3
Peterhead's local history museum with the emphasis on the fishing industry. The museum also includes an art gallery, large coin collection, Inuit artefacts and Arctic animals.

✚ **Arbuthnott Church** 55 G2
While the church is mainly 16c, the chancel dates from 1242.

🎇 **Arbuthnott House** 55 F2
This 13c fortified home of the Arbuthnott family features a 17c walled garden.

🏠 **Balbithan** 53 F2
A late 17c tower house surrounded by an attractive old-world garden.

🎇 **Balmedie Country Park** 53 G2
Situated between Balmedie and Balmedie Beach, the country park has over 150 acres (60 hectares) of grassland, dunes and sandy beach. It attracts a wide variety of seabirds.

🏠 **Barrie's House** 54 B4
This is the Kirriemuir birthplace of Sir J.M. Barrie, famous as the creator of Peter Pan. A former weaver's cottage (National Trust for Scotland), it is furnished as in Barrie's day. There is a Barrie exhibition in the adjacent house.

⚔ **Battle of Alford 1645** 52 C2
A battle site where Montrose defeated the Covenanters.

⚔ **Battle of Barra Hill 1308** 53 E1
Robert the Bruce decisively defeated John Comyn here on Christmas Eve.

⚔ **Battle of Corrichie 1562** 53 D3
The Earl of Huntly was defeated here by followers of Mary, Queen of Scots, led by Moray.

⚔ **Battle of Harlaw 1411** 53 E1
It was here that Donald, Lord of the Isles, tried to claim the Earldom of Ross and was defeated by the Earl of Mar.

⚔ **Battle of Nechtanesmere 685** 54 D5
A battle on Dunnichen Hill where Egfrith of Northumbria was killed by the Picts, thereby ending Anglian incursions into the area.

⚔ **Battle of Turiff 1639** 50 C2
This is the site of the first skirmish in the Civil War, known as the 'Trot of Turriff', where the Royalist Gordons defeated the Covenanters.

🏰 **Boyne Castle** 50 B1
Ruins of the castle, located on the Burn of Boyne near Boyne Bay.

✚ **Brechin Cathedral** 55 D4
The cathedral was built in the 13c on the site of a previous foundation in the centre of Brechin. The Brechin Round Tower (Historic Scotland) is attached.

ⓜ **Brechin Round Tower** 55 D4
An Irish-type round tower dating from the 11c (Historic Scotland) and attached to Brechin Cathedral in the centre of the city. It is one of only two such towers remaining on the Scottish mainland.

☐ **Bridge of Dee** 29 H1
Spanning the River Dee on the south approach to Aberdeen, the bridge has seven arches and dates from the 16c.

ⓜ **Brown Caterthun** 55 D3
An Iron Age fort (Historic Scotland) with four concentric entrenchments.

🍃 **Caen Lochan Nature Reserve** 54 A2
Situated in the mountains to the north west of Glendoll Lodge.

Caledonian Railway 55 E4
A tourist railway which runs 4m(6km) from the Victorian terminus at Brechin down a 1 in 70 gradient to Bridge of Dun, a junction of the former Strathmore main line.

Castle Fraser 53 E2
Built between 1575 and 1636, this baronial tower house (National Trust for Scotland) has a notable Great Hall and walled garden. It is said to be haunted.

Craig Castle 52 B1
Overlooking a wooded glen, the castle was built in the 16c and has the addition of an 18c portal and wing.

Craigievar Castle 52 C3
A 17c turreted baronial castle (National Trust for Scotland) with seven storeys and surrounded by notable grounds.

Craigston Castle 50 C2
The castle dates from the 17c.

Crathes Castle 53 E4
Built in the 16c, the castle (National Trust for Scotland) also has later additions. The gardens include early 18c yew hedges and a walled garden.

Crombie Castle 50 A2
A medieval castle to the west of Aberchirder.

Crombie Country Park 54 D5
The 250 acre (100 hectare) park surrounds the Victorian Crombie Reservoir which was styled to resemble a natural loch.

Cruickshank Botanic Garden 14 D3
Owned by the University of Aberdeen, this 11acre (4 hectare) botanic garden in Aberdeen features a rock garden, herbaceous border and an arboretum.

Cullen House 50 A1
Lying to the south west of Cullen, the house is partly 13c.

Cullerlie Stone Circle 53 E3
(Also known as Garlogie Stone Circle.)
A Bronze Age stone circle (Historic Scotland) of eight boulders with a 30 foot (9 metre) diameter, enclosing excavated burial chambers.

Culsh Earth House 52 C3
A well preserved prehistoric earth house or souterrain (Historic Scotland) at Culsh.

Deer Abbey 51 E3
Scant remains of a 13c Cistercian monastery (Historic Scotland) which are situated on the north bank of South Ugie Water.

Delgatie Castle 50 C2
(Also spelled Delgaty Castle.)
An 11c inhabited tower house containing the widest turnpike stair in Scotland and painted ceilings.

Deskford Church 50 A1
The ruin of a small medieval church (Historic Scotland), containing a carved sacrament house, on the Burn of Deskford.

Doonies Farm 31 H1
Rare breeds working farm with Shetland ponies, Clydesdale horses, cattle, sheep and pigs.

Drum Castle 53 E3
A medieval square tower (National Trust for Scotland) with Jacobean and Victorian extensionsto the west of Peterculter. The grounds contain a unique Garden of Historic Roses, 16c chapel, and woodland walks.

Duff House 50 B1
Designed by William Adam for the first Earl of Fife in 1735, Duff House (Historic Scotland) at Banff is a fine example of Georgian baroque architecture. During World War II it housed prisoners of war but now contains collections of the National Galleries of Scotland including paintings, furniture, tapestries and artefacts.

Dunnottar Castle 53 F5
Dating in part from the late 14c, this ruined fortress of the Earls of Marischal is dramatically situated on a rock promontory and was used in Zeffirelli's film of Hamlet.

Duthie Park and Winter Gardens 24 B6
This Aberdeen park by the River Dee covers 50 acres (20 hectares) and includes a boating lake. The park is renowned for the rose garden known as 'Rose Mountain' and the 2 acre Winter Gardens with a hothouse featuring exotic plants.

Dyce Symbol Stones 53 F2
Two Pictish symbol stones (Historic Scotland) which are to be found in the ruins of Dyce Old Kirk.

Eassie Sculptured Stone 54 B5
A good example of an elaborately carved early Christian monument (Historic Scotland) with a Celtic cross on one side and Pictish symbols on the reverse.

Easter Aquhorthies 53 E1
(Also known as East Aquhorthies.)
The site of an ancient recumbent stone circle (Historic Scotland) to the west of Inverurie.

Eden Castle 50 B2
Ruins of a 16c tower house on the east side of River Deveron.

Edzell Castle 55 D3
An early 16c tower house (Historic Scotland) with 17c alterations and additions by Sir David Lindsay. It includes Lindsay's formal decorated garden, or Pleasaunce. The castle was vandalised after the second Jacobite uprising.

Fasque House 55 E2
Once home of former Prime Minister William Gladstone, the interior of this 19c house is little changed since Gladstone's time. The house is surrounded by a deer park.

Finavon Castle 54 D4
Ruined 16c stronghold of the Earls of Crawford to the south of Finavon.

Finavon Doocot 54 D4
The largest dovecot (National Trust for Scotland) in Scotland with 2400 nesting boxes and dating from the 16c.

Findlater Castle   50 A1
Once an Ogilvie stronghold, this ruined 15c castle is situated on cliffs to the east of Cullen.

Fyvie Castle   50 C4
Dating from the 14c with late 16c additions, the castle has been completely restored. Notable features include a wheel staircase, Victorian earth closet and a racquet court. Fyvie castle also has a collection of armour and paintings.

Fyvie Church   50 C4
The church is noted for its stained glass, 17c panelling and Celtic stones.

Glamis Castle   54 B5
Mainly 17c but with parts of much earlier, Glamis Castle is the family home of the Earls of Strathmore and Kinghorne and was the childhood home of HM Queen Elizabeth, the Queen Mother.

Glenbuchat Castle   52 A2
A ruined Z-plan stronghold of the Gordons dating from 1590 (Historic Scotland).

Glendronach Distillery   50 B3
Located in Glen Dronach, the distillery was built in 1926. It draws its water from Dronach Burn, which has previously made its way through rich peat beds.

Glengarioch Distillery   53 F1
One of Scotland's oldest distilleries, Glengarioch was founded in 1797 at Oldmeldrum. It is housed in a granite building at one end of the Garioch valley and draws its water from springs on Percock Hill.

Gordon Highlanders Regimental Museum   23 E4
Commemorating the regiment first raised by the Duke of Gordon in 1794, the museum displays uniforms, colours, weapons and paintings. It is housed in the former home of Victorian artist Sir George Reid in south west Aberdeen.

Grampian Transport Museum   52 C2
Historic vehicles of every description are displayed in this museum at Alford. Attractions include a driving simulator and a video bus presenting the history of road transport and motor sport.

Haddo House   51 D4
An elegant mansion of 1731 (National Trust for Scotland) designed by William Adam. Haddo House is the Seat of the Marquess of Aberdeen. It has a beautiful library and houses a permanent exhibition of James Giles' paintings. There is a terraced rose garden.

Haughton House Country Park   52 C2
Surrounding 19c Haughton House, the 48 acre (19 hectare) country park consists chiefly of woodland with gardens, an aviary and an adventure playground. The visitor centre has displays on local farming life and natural history.

Hazlehead Park   22 A4
Comprising woodland and rose gardens, this Aberdeen park also contains a pets corner, aquarium, walk-in aviary and maze.

House of Dun   55 E4
An 18c Palladian house (National Trust for Scotland) designed by William Adam and built for David Erskine, Lord Dun.

Huntly Castle   50 A3
The remains of a Gordon stronghold (Historic Scotland) beside the River Deveron to the north of Huntley. Partly 12c but mainly 16c, Huntly Castle has notable heraldic sculptures and inscribed stone friezes.

Kildrummy Castle   52 B2
A ruined 13c courtyard castle (Historic Scotland), a former stronghold of the Earls of Mar which was dismantled after the Jacobite rising of 1715. The gardens are notable for shrubs and alpines, and include water gardens and an ancient quarry.

King's College Visitor Centre   14 D4
A multi-media exhibition of Aberdeen University's 500 year history, housed in the Victorian King's Library Building, Old Aberdeen.

Kinkell Church   53 E2
The ruins of a 16c parish church with a fine sacrament house (Historic Scotland), to the south of Inverurie on the east side of the River Don. The grave slab of Gilbert of Greenlaw who was killed in battle in 1411 is to be found here.

Kinneff Church   55 G2
Part of the church formed the hiding place for the Scottish crown jewels smuggled from Dunnottar castle whilst under seige from Cromwell in 1651. The present church dates from 1738.

Leith Hall   52 C1
Home of the head of the Leith family since 1650, the 17c house (National Trust for Scotland) is built round a central courtyard. It contains a collection of military memorabilia and there are both formal and informal gardens.

Loanhead Stone Circle   53 E1
A Bronze Age stone circle (Historic Scotland) which encloses a ring cairn. There is also a small burial enclosure nearby.

Loch of Strathbeg   51 F2
Situated behind Strathbeg Bay, this land-locked coastal lagoon is 2miles (3km) long and has a RSPB reserve.

Loirston Country Park   30 B3
This 620 acre (250 hectare) country park to the south east of Aberdeen harbour has coastal walks and includes Girdle Ness lighthouse. It attracts a wide variety of seabirds and other wildlife.

Maiden Stone   53 E1
A 9c red granite Pictish symbol stone (Historic Scotland), with Pictish symbols carved on one side and a Celtic cross on the other. Maiden Stone is 10 feet (3 metres) high.

Marischal Museum   5 D1
Aberdeen University's anthropological museum in central Aberdeen with displays illustrating the archaeology and folk history of north east Scotland. Egyptian antiquities are amongst the other collections.

⊡ **Meffan Institute**   **54 C4**
Museum and art gallery at Forfar with Neolithic, Pictish and Celtic exhibits, and a section on 17c witch-hunting.

▥ **Meigle Sculptured Stones**   **54 A5**
Christian and Pictish inscribed stones (Historic Scotland) at Meigle. In the Meigle Museum, are housed approximately 30 other stones from the area, dating from 7c-10c.

▥ **Memsie Cairn**   **51 E1**
Possibly dating from the Bronze Age, this is a fine example of a large stone cairn (Historic Scotland).

▥ **Montrose Museum and Art Gallery**   **55 F4**
Montrose's local history museum with maritime and natural history exhibits and including the art gallery.

▥ **Muchalls Castle**   **53 F4**
The 17c castle was destroyed by fire in the second Jacobite uprising and later rebuilt.

▥ **Museum of Scottish Lighthouses**   **51 E1**
The museum is located at Kinnaird Head at Fraserburgh and commemorates Scottish lighthouses. Housed in the first lighthouse (Historic Scotland) built by the Northern Lighthouse Company in 1787, itself contained within a 16c castle built for the Fraser family, the museum includes the history of the Stevenson family, designers of many Scottish lighthouses.

▥ **Peel Ring of Lumphanan**   **52 C3**
A moated medieval motte (Historic Scotland) to the south west of Lumphanan, where it is said Macbeth made his last stand. The structure is 120 feet (36.5 metres) in diameter by 18 feet (5.5 metres) high.

⊡ **Peterhead Maritime Heritage Centre**   **51 G3**
Illustrating the importance of maritime industries to Peterhead, the centre has displays on fishing, whaling and the oil industries.

▥ **Picardy Stone**   **50 B4**
The stone dates back from the 7c or 8c and contains Pictish inscriptions (Historic Scotland).

▥ **Pitcaple Castle**   **53 E1**
Lying to the north east of Pitcaple, a 16c Z-plan castle which was renovated in the 19c.

▩ **Pitmedden Garden**   **53 F1**
National Trust for Scotland property which includes a 17c garden designed by Sir Alexander Seton, Baron of Pitmedden, and a Museum of Farming Life.

▥ **Pitsligo Castle**   **51 E1**
Ruined castle of the Forbes family, dating from 1424, and now partly renovated.

☐ **Provost Ross's House**   **5 D2**
15c home of a former Lord Provost of Aberdeen at Shiprow in Aberdeen. Entered from Aberdeen Maritime Museum, it now houses a National Trust for Scotland visitor centre.

☐ **Provost Skene's House**   **5 D2**
A fine example of early burgh architecture in Guestrow, Aberdeen. Dating from the 16c, the house contains furnished period rooms, painted ceilings, a costume gallery and local history displays.

▥ **Red Castle**   **55 E4**
(Also known as Ederdover Castle.)
Ruins of a 16c L-plan tower house on the south bank of the Lunan Water estuary to the north east of Inverkeilor.

⊞ **Restenneth Priory**   **54 C4**
The ruined chancel and tower of a 12c Augustinian priory church (Historic Scotland). The lower part of the tower is early Romanesque in style.

☐ **St. Machar's Cathedral**   **14 D3**
A twin-towered 15c granite fortified cathedral built on an ancient site of worship in Aberdeen. The nave, dated 1520, is still used as a parish church. Features include a 16c oak heraldic ceiling and notable stained glass. The ruined transepts (Historic Scotland) contain the tomb of Bishop Dunbar.

⊞ **St. Mary's Kirk**   **52 B1**
Roofless medieval parish church (Historic Scotland) at Auchindoir featuring a carved early Romanesque doorway and an early 14c sacrament house.

▥ **St. Orland's Stone**   **54 C5**
Symbol stone (Historic Scotland) depicting hunting and boating scenes.

☐ **Satrosphere**   **5 E1**
Hands-on science and technology discovery centre in Aberdeen.

▥ **Slains Castle**   **51 G4**
Site of a 19c castle, now demolished, on a granite headland above Port Errol.

☐ **Storybook Glen**   **33 G5**
Nursery and fairytale fantasyland and leisure park for children in landscaped gardens to the east of Kirkton of Maryculter.

☐ **The Blairs Museum**   **34 A1**
Scottish Roman Catholic heritage collection of decorative art, church plate, and embroidered vestments with artefacts relating to the Stewarts and Mary Queen of Scots. The collection is housed in the former Roman Catholic school, Blairs College.

▥ **Tolquhon Castle**   **53 F1**
The remains of a pink sandstone medieval castle (Historic Scotland) built for the Forbes family. Situated in a wooded glen to the north west of Pitmedden, the ruin includes a 15c-16c tower and an ornamented gatehouse.

▥ **Tomnaverie Stone Circle**   **52 B3**
Stones dating from 1800-1600 BC (Historic Scotland) on a rocky knoll to the south east of Tarland.

▥ **Towie Barclay Castle**   **50 C3**
Remains of a ruined 16c castle to the south of Mains of Towie.

▥ **White Caterthun**   **54 D3**
Well-preserved Iron Age fort (Historic Scotland) with a massive stone rampart.

48 Key to Road Map Symbols

M5	Motorway
30 – 29	Motorway junctions (full, limited access)
● Maidstone / Birch Sarn	Motorway service areas (off road, full, limited access)
A48	Primary route dual/single
A30	'A' road dual/single
B1403	'B' road dual/single
	Minor road
	Restricted access due to road conditions or private ownership
Poole 2½ hrs (3 hrs)	Car ferry route with journey times; daytime and (night-time)
—o—	Railway line and station
	Railway tunnel

= = = = = = = =	Road projected or under construction
⊗	Multi-level junction
●○●○◎○◎○	Roundabout
10	Road distance in miles
)▪▪▪▪(	Road tunnel
→	Steep hill (arrows point downhill)
✕ Toll	Level crossing/Toll
✈	Airport with scheduled services
Ⓗ	Heliport
⊢⊣⊢⊣	Canal / dry canal / canal tunnel

	Built up area
□ ▫ ▫	Town / Village / Other settlement
Peterhead	Primary route destination
	Woodland
	Beach
·468	Spot height (metres)
▲491	Summit height (metres)
	Lake / Dam / River / Waterfall
▶15	Page continuation number

▪·▪·▪·▪	National boundary
▪·▪·▪·▪	County / Unitary Authority boundary
▪▪▪▪▪	National / Regional Park
	Forest Park boundary
Danger Zone	Military range
³30	National Grid reference

More details of the places of interest shown on the mapping can be found on pages 44-47

t / *i*	Tourist information office (all year / seasonal)
⊷ ···•···	Preserved railway
�m	Ancient monument
✚	Ecclesiastical building
⌂	Historic house (with or without garden)
⌂	Museum / Art gallery
£	Factory shop village
⊠¹⁷³⁸	Battlefield
⚏	Castle
✿	Garden
⊞	Country park
▶	Nature reserve
✾	Theme park
✂	Racecourse
✗	Major sports venue
⚑	Motor racing circuit
🐘	Wildlife park or Zoo
★	Other interesting feature
⚐	Golf course
(NT) (NTS)	National Trust property / National Trust for Scotland

land below	0	165	490	985	1640	2295	2950	feet
water	sea level 0	50	150	300	500	700	900	metres

SCALE: 4 miles to 1 inch approx (10km to 4cm)

0	4	8	12	16 miles
0	5	10	15	20	25 kilometres

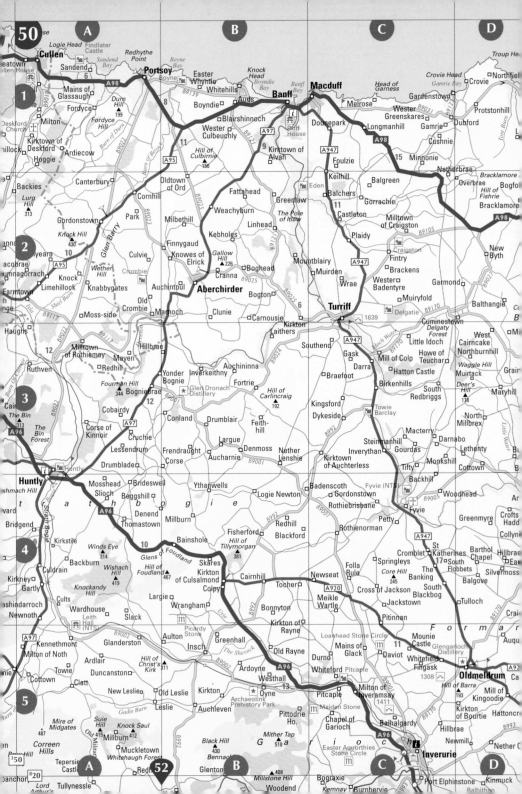

General Abbreviations

All	Alley	Conv	Convent	Gdn	Garden	Ms	Mews	Sec	Secondary
Allot	Allotments	Cor	Corner	Gdns	Gardens	Mt	Mount	Shop	Shopping
Amb	Ambulance	Coron	Coroners	Govt	Government	Mus	Museum	Sq	Square
App	Approach	Cors	Corners	Gra	Grange	N	North	St.	Saint
Arc	Arcade	Cotts	Cottages	Grd	Ground	NT	National	St	Street
Av/Ave	Avenue	Cov	Covered	Grds	Grounds		Trust	Sta	Station
Bdy	Broadway	Crem	Crematorium	Grn	Green	Nat	National	Sts	Streets
Bk	Bank	Cres	Crescent	Grns	Greens	PH	Public House	Sub	Subway
Bldgs	Buildings	Ct	Court	Gro	Grove	PO	Post Office	Swim	Swimming
Boul	Boulevard	Cts	Courts	Gros	Groves	Par	Parade	TA	Territorial
Bowl	Bowling	Ctyd	Courtyard	Gt	Great	Pas	Passage		Army
Br/Bri	Bridge	Dep	Depot	Ho	House	Pav	Pavilion	TH	Town Hall
C of E	Church of	Dev	Development	Hos	Houses	Pk	Park	Tenn	Tennis
	England	Dr	Drive	Hosp	Hospital	Pl	Place	Ter	Terrace
Cath	Cathedral	Dws	Dwellings	Hts	Heights	Pol	Police	Thea	Theatre
Cem	Cemetery	E	East	Ind	Industrial	Prec	Precinct	Trd	Trading
Cen	Central,	Ed	Education	Int	International	Prim	Primary	Twr	Tower
	Centre	Elec	Electricity	Junct	Junction	Prom	Promenade	Twrs	Towers
Cft	Croft	Embk	Embankment	La	Lane	Pt	Point	Uni	University
Cfts	Crofts	Est	Estate	Las	Lanes	Quad	Quadrant	Up	Upper
Ch	Church	Ex	Exchange	Lib	Library	RC	Roman	Vil	Villa, Villas
Chyd	Churchyard	Exhib	Exhibition	Lo	Lodge		Catholic	Vw	View
Cin	Cinema	FB	Footbridge	Lwr	Lower	Rd	Road	W	West
Circ	Circus	FC	Football Club	Mag	Magistrates	Rds	Roads	Wd	Wood
Cl/Clo	Close	Fld	Field	Mans	Mansions	Rec	Recreation	Wds	Woods
Co	County	Flds	Fields	Mem	Memorial	Res	Reservoir	Wf	Wharf
Coll	College	Fm	Farm	Mid	Middle	Ri	Rise	Wk	Walk
Comm	Community	Gall	Gallery	Mkt	Market	S	South	Wks	Works
Comn	Common	Gar	Garage	Mkts	Markets	Sch	School	Yd	Yard

District Abbreviations

Bield.	Bieldside	Dane.	Danestone
Br.Don	Bridge of Don	Kings.	Kingswells
Bucks.	Bucksburn	Newt.	Newtonhill
Co.Bay	Cove Bay	Port.	Portlethen

Post Town Abbreviations

Mill.	Milltimber
Peter.	Peterculter
Stone.	Stonehaven
Westh.	Westhill

This index contains streets that are not named on the map due to insufficient space. For each of these cases the nearest street that does appear on the map is also listed in *italics*.

Name		
Abbey La. (Torry) AB11	25	E4
Abbey Pl. AB11	25	E4
Abbey Rd. AB11	25	E4
Abbey Sq. AB11	25	E4
Abbots Pl. AB12	30	B1
Abbotsford La. AB11	24	B4
Abbotsford Pl. AB11	24	B4
Ferryhill Rd.		
Abbotshall Cres. (Cults) AB15	28	A2
Abbotshall Dr. (Cults) AB15	28	A2
Abbotshall Gdns. (Cults) AB15	28	A2
Abbotshall Pl. (Cults) AB15	28	A2
Abbotshall Rd. (Cults) AB15	28	B1
Abbotshall Ter. (Cults) AB15	28	A2
Abbotshall Wk. (Cults) AB15	28	A2
Abbotswell Cres. AB12	30	B1
Abbotswell Dr. AB12	30	A1
Abbotswell Rd. AB12	30	C1
Aberdeen Airport (Dyce) AB21	6	D4
Aberdeen Mkt. AB11	24	C2
Union St.		
Aberdeen Offshore Technology Pk. (Br.Don) AB23	11	G5
Aberdeen Science & Technology Pk. (Br.Don) AB22	10	C6
Aberdon Ct. AB24	14	C3
Coningham Ter.		
Aberdon Ho. Ct. AB24	14	C3
Coningham Rd.		
Abergeldie Rd. AB10	23	H5
Abergeldie Ter. AB10	23	H5
Aboyne Gdns. AB10	29	F1
Aboyne Pl. AB10	29	F2
Aboyne Rd. AB10	29	F2
Aboyne Ter. AB10	29	G2
Academy St. AB11	5	C3
Acorn Pl. (Port.) AB12	38	D5
Adelphi AB11	5	D2
Adelphi La. AB11 *Adelphi*	24	C2
Advocates Rd. AB24	15	E6
Affleck Pl. AB11	24	B3
Marywell St.		
Affleck St. AB11	5	C3
Airside Business Pk. (Dyce) AB21	6	C3
Airyhall Av. AB15	22	C6
Airyhall Cres. AB15	22	C6
Airyhall Dr. AB15	22	C6
Airyhall Gdns. AB15	22	D6
Airyhall Pl. AB15	22	D6
Airyhall Rd. AB15	28	C1
Airyhall Ter. AB15	22	D6
Albert La. AB25	23	G3
Albert Pl. AB25	4	A2
Albert Quay AB11	5	E3
Albert St. AB25	4	A2
Albert Ter. AB10	4	A3
Albert Wk. AB10	23	H3
Albert Ter.		
Albury Gdns. AB11	24	B4
Albury Rd.		
Albury Mans. AB11	24	B4
Albury Rd.		
Albury Pl. AB11	24	B4
Albury Rd. AB11	24	A4
Albyn Gro. AB10	4	A3
Albyn La. AB10	4	A3
Albyn Pl. AB10	4	A3
Albyn Ter. AB10	4	A3
Alder Dr. (Port.) AB12	38	C5
Alexander Dr. AB24	14	B2
Alexander Ter. AB24	14	B3
Alford La. AB10	4	B3
Alford Pl. AB10	24	A3
Albyn Pl.		
Allan St. AB10	23	H4
Allenvale Gdns. AB10	24	A6
Allenvale Rd. AB10	24	A6
Allison Cl. (Co.Bay) AB12	30	D5
Alma Rd. AB23	11	F6
Altens Fm. Rd. (Nigg) AB12	30	D2
Altens Ind. Est. AB12	30	C4
Altonrea Gdns. (Dyce) AB21	7	G3
Anderson Av. AB24	14	A3
Anderson Dr. AB15	23	E4
Anderson Dr. (Newt.), Stone. AB39	41	E4
Anderson Rd. AB24	13	H3
Angusfield Av. AB15	22	D3
Angusfield La. AB15	22	D3
Ann St. AB25	4	B1
Annat Bk. AB12	31	E5
Annfield Ter. AB10	23	G4
Arbroath La. AB12	30	B2
Arbroath Pl. AB12	30	C2
Arbroath Way AB12	30	B2
Ardarroch Cl. AB24	15	F5
Ardarroch Rd.		
Ardarroch Pl. AB24	15	F5
Ardarroch Rd. AB24	15	E5
Ardbeck Pl., Peter. AB14	33	E2
Ardlair Ter. (Dyce) AB21	7	G2
Argyll Cl. AB21	6	C5
Argyll Cres. AB25	23	G1
Argyll Pl. (Port.) AB12	39	E2
Argyll Pl. AB25	23	G1
Argyll Rd. (Dyce) AB21	6	C5
Arnage Cres. AB16	13	F6
Arnage Dr. AB16	13	E6
Arnage Gdns. AB16	13	F6
Arnage Pl. AB16	13	F6
Arnage Ter. AB16	13	F6
Arnhall Business Pk., Westh. AB32	17	E5
Arnhall Cres., Westh. AB32	17	F5
Arnhall Dr., Westh. AB32	17	F5
Arnot Pl. (Port.) AB12	39	G4
Arran Av. AB16	12	B6
Aryburn Row (Dyce) AB21	7	G3

Name	Page	Grid
Ash Ct. (Port.) AB12	38	C4
Ash Gro. (Port.) AB12	38	D5
Ash Pl. (Port.) AB12	38	D5
Ash-hill Dr. AB16	13	H5
Ash-hill Pl. AB16	14	A5
Rosehill Dr.		
Ash-hill Rd. AB16	14	A5
Ash-hill Way AB16	14	A5
Ashdale Cl., Westh. AB32	16	D4
Ashdale Ct., Westh. AB32	17	E4
Ashdale Dr.		
Ashdale Dr., Westh. AB32	17	E4
Ashfield Rd. (Cults) AB15	28	B2
Ashgrove Av. AB25	14	B5
Ashgrove Ct. AB25	14	A5
Ashgrove Gdns. N. AB16	13	G6
Ashgrove Gdns. S. AB16	13	G6
Ashgrove Pl. AB16	13	G6
Ashgrove Rd. AB16	14	B6
Ashgrove Rd. W. AB16	13	G6
Ashgrove Rd. W. AB25	13	G6
Ashley Gdns. AB10	23	G4
Ashley Gro. AB10	23	H4
Ashley La. AB10	23	G4
Ashley Pk. Dr. AB10	23	G4
Ashley Pk. La. AB10	23	H4
Ashley Pk. N. AB10	23	G4
Ashley Pk. S. AB10	23	H4
Ashley Rd. AB10	23	H4
Ashtown Pl. (Bucks.) AB21	12	B2
Newhills Av.		
Ashtown Wk. (Bucks.) AB21	12	B2
Ashvale Cl. AB10	24	A3
Cuparstone Row		
Ashvale Pl. AB10	4	A3
Ashwood Av. (Br.Don) AB22	10	B3
Ashwood Circle (Br.Don) AB22	10	B2
Ashwood Cres. (Br.Don) AB22	10	A3
Ashwood Dr. (Br.Don) AB22	10	B3
Ashwood Gdns. (Br.Don) AB22	10	B2
Ashwood Gra. (Br.Don) AB22	10	B3
Ashwood Ms. (Br.Don) AB22	10	B2
Ashwood Par. (Br.Don) AB22	10	A2
Ashwood Pk. (Br.Don) AB22	10	B3
Ashwood Pl. (Br.Don) AB22	10	A2
Ashwood Rd. (Br.Don) AB22	10	B2
Aspen Gro., Westh. AB32	16	C5
Aspen Way (Port.) AB12	38	D5
Auchinleck Cres. AB24	14	B2
Auchinleck Rd. AB24	14	B2
Auchinyell Gdns. AB10	29	F1
Auchinyell Rd. AB10	29	F1
Auchinyell Ter. AB10	29	F1
Auchlea Pl. AB16	22	A1
Auchlea Rd. AB16	22	A1
Auchlossan Ct. (Br.Don) AB22	14	D1
Davan Pk.		
Auchmill Rd. (Bucks.) AB21	12	D1
Auchmill Ter. (Bucks.) AB21	13	F2
Auchriny Circle (Bucks.) AB21	7	F6
Auckland Pl. AB24	15	E5
Merkland St.		
Auldearn Gdns. AB12	30	B2
Auldearn Pl. AB12	30	B2
Auldearn Rd. AB12	30	B2
Aulton Ct. AB24	15	F3
Avon Pl. (Dyce) AB21	7	F3

B

Name	Page	Grid
Back Hilton Rd. AB25	14	B5
Back Wynd AB10	5	C2
Badentoy Av. (Badentoy Ind. Est.) AB12	38	B1
Badentoy Business Cen. (Port.) AB12	38	A1
Badentoy Cres. (Badentoy Ind. Est.) AB12	38	A1
Badentoy Pk. Ind. Est.	38	B1
Badentoy Pl. (Badentoy Ind. Est.) AB12	38	B1
Badentoy Rd. (Badentoy Ind. Est.) AB12	38	C2
Baillieswell Gro. (Bield.) AB15	27	F3
Baillieswells Cres. (Bield.) AB15	27	F3
Baillieswells Dr. (Bield.) AB15	27	F3
Baillieswells Pl. (Bield.) AB15	27	F3
Baillieswells Rd. (Bield.) AB15	27	F3

Name	Page	Grid
Baillieswells Ter. (Bield.) AB15	27	F3
Bairds Brae (Cults) AB15	28	C1
Baker Pl. AB25	24	A1
Baker St.		
Baker St. AB25	4	B1
Balfron Pl. AB15	22	D2
Balgownie Brae (Br.Don) AB22	14	C1
Balgownie Ct. AB24	15	E3
Balgownie Cres. (Br.Don) AB23	15	E1
Balgownie Dr. (Br.Don) AB22	14	B1
Balgownie Gdns. (Br.Don) AB22	14	C1
Balgownie Pl. (Br.Don) AB22	14	B1
Balgownie Rd. (Br.Don) AB22	14	D1
Balgownie Rd. (Br.Don) AB23	15	E1
Balgownie Way (Br.Don) AB22	14	B1
Balloch Way AB21	7	G2
Balmoral Ct. AB10	24	A5
South Mile End		
Balmoral Pl. AB10	23	H5
Balmoral Rd. AB10	24	A5
Balmoral Ter. AB10	23	H5
Balnagask Av. AB11	25	F5
Balnagask Circle		
Balnagask Circle AB11	25	F5
Balnagask Pl. AB11	25	F4
Balnagask Rd. AB11	25	E5
Balnagask Wk. AB11	25	E5
Farquhar Rd.		
Baltic Pl. AB11	5	E2
Baltic St. AB11	5	E2
Bank St. AB11	24	B4
Bank St. (Woodside) AB24	14	A3
Bankhead Av. (Bucks.) AB21	12	B1
Bankhead Ind. Est. (Bucks.) AB21	12	C1
Bankhead Rd. (Bucks.) AB21	8	C6
Bannerman Pl. AB16	12	D3
Bannermill Pl. AB24	24	D1
Beach Boul.		
Bannermill St. AB11	24	D1
Cotton St.		
Barbour Brae (Br.Don) AB22	10	B6
Barclayhill Pl. (Port.) AB12	39	E2
Barkmill Rd. AB25	14	B5
Ashgrove Rd.		
Barra Wk. AB16	22	A1
Barringer La., Westh. AB32	17	F4
Barron St. AB24	14	B3
Sandilands Dr.		
Barrowstone Pl. AB16	22	A1
Derbeth Cres.		
Barvas Wk. AB16	12	B6
Bath St. AB11	24	B2
Windmill Brae		
Battock Pl. AB11	24	D5
Baxter Ct. AB11	25	F4
Baxter Pl.		
Baxter Pl. AB11	25	F4
Baxter St. AB11	25	F4
Bayview Ct. AB24	15	F4
Bayview Rd. AB15	23	F3
Bayview Rd. S. AB15	23	F4
Beach Boul. AB24	5	E1
Beachview Ct. AB24	15	F3
Beaconhill Rd., Mill. AB13	26	D5
Beaconsfield Pl. AB15	23	F3
Beattie Av. AB25	14	B5
Beattie Pl. AB25	14	B5
Elder Pl.		
Bedford Av. AB24	14	C4
Bedford Pl. AB24	14	C5
Bedford Rd. AB24	14	C5
Beech Rd. AB16	13	F5
Beech Rd., Westh. AB32	16	D5
Beechgrove Av. AB15	23	G2
Beechgrove Ct. AB15	23	G2
Beechgrove Ter.		
Beechgrove Gdns. AB15	23	G1
Beechgrove Pl. AB15	23	G2
Beechgrove Ter. AB15	23	G2
Beechhill Gdns. AB15	22	D6
Beechwood Av. AB16	13	H6
Beechwood Cl., Westh. AB32	16	C5
Beechwood Gdns.		
Beechwood Ct. AB16	13	G6
Castleton Dr.		
Beechwood Gdns., Westh. AB32	16	C5
Beechwood Pl. AB16	13	H5
Beechwood Pl., Westh. AB32	16	C4

Name	Page	Grid
Beechwood Rd. AB16	13	H5
Beechwood Wk. AB16	13	H5
Belgrave Ter. AB25	4	A2
Bellenden Wk., Mill. AB13	26	A6
Bellfield Rd. AB16	12	D6
Bellfield Rd. (Br.Don) AB23	11	E6
Belmont Gdns. AB25	14	B5
Belmont Rd. AB25	14	C5
Belmont St. AB10	5	C2
Belmuir Gdns. (Dyce) AB21	7	F2
Belrorie Circle (Dyce) AB21	7	G2
Belvidere Cres. AB25	4	A2
Belvidere La. (Cults) AB15	28	A3
Belvidere Rd. (Cults) AB15	27	H3
Belvidere St. AB25	4	A1
Benbecula Rd. AB16	12	B6
Berneray Pl. AB16	22	A1
Berry St. AB25	5	D1
Berryden Business Pk. AB25	14	C6
Berryden Rd.		
Berryden Rd. AB25	14	C6
Berryhill Pl. (Newt.), Stone. AB39	40	D4
Berrymoss Ct. (Dyce) AB21	7	G2
Balloch Way		
Berrymuir Pl. (Port.) AB12	38	C5
Berrymuir Rd. (Port.) AB12	38	C5
Berrymuir Wynd (Port.) AB12	38	C5
Berrywell Gdns. (Dyce) AB21	7	F2
Berrywell Pl. (Dyce) AB21	7	F2
Berrywell Rd. (Dyce) AB21	7	F2
Berrywell Wk. (Dyce) AB21	7	F2
Bervie Brow AB12	30	D5
Bethany Gdns. AB11	24	A4
Bethlin Ms. (Kings.) AB15	18	D4
Bettridge Rd. (Newt.), Stone. AB39	41	E4
Binghill Cres., Mill. AB13	26	B5
Binghill Dr., Mill. AB13	26	B4
Binghill Hedges, Mill. AB13	26	B4
Binghill Pk., Mill. AB13	26	C5
Binghill Rd., Mill. AB13	26	C4
Binghill Rd. N., Mill. AB13	26	B4
Binghill Rd. W., Mill. AB13	26	B4
Birch Av., Westh. AB32	16	D5
Birch Rd. AB16	13	H5
Rowan Rd.		
Birchfield Pl. (Co.Bay) AB12	37	G1
Redwood Cres.		
Birkhall Par. AB16	13	E5
Birkhall Pl. AB16	13	E5
Bishopsloch Row (Dyce) AB21	7	G3
Blackburn Pl. (Old Aberdeen) AB24	14	D4
High St.		
Blackfriars St. AB25	4	C1
Blackhills Ct., Westh. AB32	16	C4
Blackhills Pl.		
Blackhills Pl., Westh. AB32	16	C4
Blackhills Way, Westh. AB32	16	C4
Blackhills Pl.		
Blacklaws Brae, Westh. AB32	16	D2
Blackness Av. (Altens Ind. Est.) AB12	31	F4
Blackness Rd. (Altens Ind. Est.) AB12	31	F4
Blacks La. AB11	5	E3
Blacksmiths Cft. (Bucks.) AB21	13	E2
Cairnfield Pl.		
Blackthorn Cres. AB16	13	H5
Blaikies Quay AB11	5	E2
Bleachfield Rd. (Br.Don) AB22	10	C6
Silverburn Rd.		
Blenheim La. AB25	23	G2
Blenheim Pl. AB25	23	G2
Bloomfield Ct. AB10	24	A5
Bloomfield Pl. AB10	24	A4
Bloomfield Rd. AB10	24	A5
Boa Vista Pl. AB24	14	D5
Spital		
Bob Cooney Ct. AB25	14	C6
Bodachra Path (Br.Don) AB22	10	C6
Bodachra Pl.		
Bodachra Pl. (Br.Don) AB22	10	C6
Bodachra Rd. (Br.Don) AB22	10	C6
Boddie Pl. AB24	15	E6
Bon Accord Cres. AB11	4	C3
Bon Accord Cres. La. AB11	24	B3
Bon Accord Cres.		
Bon Accord La. AB11	4	C3
Bon Accord Sq. AB11	4	C3
Bon Accord St. AB11	4	C3
Bon Accord Ter. AB11	4	B3

Bonnymuir Pl. AB15	23	G1
Bonnyview Dr. AB16	12	D3
Bonnyview Pl. AB16	12	D3
Bonnyview Rd. AB16	12	D3
Bonnyview Dr.		
Booth Pl. (Bucks.) AB21	12	C1
Kingsway		
Borrowstone Pl. AB16	12	C6
Sheddocksley Dr.		
Boswell Av. (Port.) AB12	38	C3
Boswell Rd. (Port.) AB12	38	C3
Boswell Wk. (Port.) AB12	38	C3
Boswell Way (Port.) AB12	38	C3
Boswell Wynd (Port.) AB12	38	C3
Bourtree Av. (Port.) AB12	38	C5
Boyd Orr Av. AB12	30	A4
Boyd Orr Cl. AB12	30	A4
Boyd Orr Pl. AB12	29	H4
Boyd Orr Wk. AB12	29	H4
Bracken Rd. (Port.) AB12	38	D3
Bradley Ter. AB24	14	C3
Braecroft Av., Westh. AB32	17	E4
Braecroft Cres., Westh. AB32	17	E4
Braecroft Dr., Westh. AB32	17	E4
Braefoot Rd. AB16	14	A5
Braehead (Br.Don) AB22	10	D6
Glashieburn Way		
Braehead Ter., Mill. AB13	26	B5
Braehead Way (Br.Don) AB22	10	C6
Braemar Pl. AB10	23	H5
Braeside Av. AB15	29	E1
Braeside Pl. AB15	22	D6
Braeside Ter. AB15	29	E1
Bramble Brae AB16	13	G4
Brander Pl. (Dane.) AB22	14	A1
Brebner Cres. AB16	12	D4
Brebner Ter. AB16	12	D4
Brebner's Ct. AB11	24	C2
Justice St.		
Brent Rd. (Dyce) AB21	6	D4
Bressay Brae AB15	22	A1
Brewery La. AB24	14	D4
High St.		
Bridge of Dee AB10	29	H1
Bridge of Dee AB10	29	H1
Bridge of Don AB24	15	F2
Bridge of Don Ind. Est. AB23	11	E5
Bridge Pl. AB11	24	B2
Bridge St.		
Bridge St. AB11	5	C2
Bridge St. (Woodside) AB24	13	H3
Great Northern Rd.		
Brierfield Rd. AB16	13	H5
Brierfield Ter. AB16	13	G5
Brig o' Balgownie AB24	15	E1
Bright St. AB11	24	B5
Brighton Gra., Peter. AB14	32	D3
Brighton Pl. AB10	23	G4
Brighton Pl., Peter. AB14	32	D3
Brimmond Ct. AB11	25	F5
Balnagask Circle		
Brimmond Ct., Westh. AB32	16	D5
Brimmond Cres., Westh. AB32	16	D5
Brimmond Dr., Westh. AB32	16	D5
Brimmond La., Westh. AB32	16	D5
Brimmond Pl. AB11	24	D5
Brimmond Pl., Westh. AB32	16	D5
Brimmond Vw. (Bucks.) AB21	8	B5
Brimmond Wk., Westh. AB32	16	D5
Brimmond Way, Westh. AB32	16	D5
Brimmondside (Bucks.) AB21	12	A2
Broad St. AB10	5	D2
Broaddykes (Kings.) AB15	18	D4
Broaddykes Cl. (Kings.) AB15	18	D4
Broaddykes Cres. (Kings.) AB15	18	D5
Broaddykes Dr. (Kings.) AB15	18	C5
Broaddykes Pl. (Kings.) AB15	18	C4
Broaddykes Vw. (Kings.) AB15	18	D5
Broaddykes Way (Kings.) AB15	18	C5
Broaddykes Dr.		
Broadfold Dr. (Br.Don) AB23	11	E6
Broadfold Rd. (Br.Don) AB23	11	E5
Broadfold Ter. (Br.Don) AB23	11	E6
Gordon Pl.		
Broadhaven Rd. (Port.) AB12	39	G4
Broadlands Gdns., Westh. AB32	16	B4
Old Skene Rd.		
Broadstraik Av., Westh. AB32	16	B5
Broadstraik Dr., Westh. AB32	16	B5
Straik Rd.		
Broadstraik Pl., Westh. AB32	16	B5
Broadstraik Av.		
Brodiach Ct., Westh. AB32	17	F4
Brodinch Pl. AB16	12	D6
Brodinch Rd. AB16	12	D6
Brooke Cres. (Br.Don) AB23	11	E4
Broom Pk. AB15	27	H2
Broomfield Pk. (Port.) AB12	38	C4
Broomfield Rd. (Port.) AB12	38	C4
Broomhill Av. AB10	23	H6
Broomhill Pk. AB10	23	H5
Broomhill Rd.		
Broomhill Pl. AB10	23	H6
Broomhill Rd. AB10	23	H5
Broomhill Ter. AB10	23	H6
Brough Pl. AB25	14	A5
Carnie Dr.		
Brown St. AB24	14	A3
Bruce Ho. AB15	22	B3
Hazlehead Rd.		
Bruce Wk. AB12	30	C3
Brucklay Ct. (Dyce) AB21	7	G3
Brunswick Pl. AB11	24	B5
Bruntland Ct. (Port.) AB12	38	D4
Bruntland Pl. (Port.) AB12	39	E4
Bruntland Rd. (Port.) AB12	38	D4
Buchan Pl. AB11	25	F5
Buchan Rd. AB11	25	F5
Buchan Rd. (Dyce) AB21	6	C3
Buchan Ter. AB11	25	F5
Buchanan Gdns. AB12	30	B3
Buchanan Pl. AB12	30	B3
Buchanan Rd. AB12	30	B3
Buckie Av. (Br.Don) AB22	10	A5
Buckie Cl. (Br.Don) AB22	10	A5
Buckie Cres. (Br.Don) AB22	10	A5
Buckie Gro. (Br.Don) AB22	10	B5
Buckie Rd. (Br.Don) AB22	10	A5
Buckie Wk. (Br.Don) AB22	10	A5
Buckie Wynd (Br.Don) AB22	10	A5
Bucklerburn Cl., Peter. AB14	32	C1
Bucklerburn Dr., Peter. AB14	32	D2
Bucklerburn Pk., Peter. AB14	32	D2
Bucklerburn Pl., Peter. AB14	32	D2
Bucklerburn Rd., Peter. AB14	32	D1
Bucklerburn Vw., Peter. AB14	32	D1
Bucklerburn Wynd, Peter. AB14	32	C2
Bunstane Ter. (Co.Bay) AB12	37	G1
Spark Ter.		
Bunzeach Pl. (Dyce) AB21	7	G2
Ardlair Ter.		
Burnbank Pl. AB11	25	E5
Burnbank Ter. AB11	25	E5
Burnbanks Village (Co. Bay) AB12	31	F4
Burnbrae Av. AB16	22	C1
Burnbrae Cres. AB16	22	C1
Burnbrae Pl. AB16	22	C1
Burnbutts Cres. (Co.Bay) AB12	37	G1
Burndale Rd. (Bucks.) AB21	8	C6
Burnett Pl. AB24	14	B4
Burnieboozle Cres. AB15	22	B5
Burnieboozle Pl. AB15	22	C5
Burns Gdns. AB15	23	F4
Burns Rd. AB15	23	F4
Burnside Dr. (Dyce) AB21	7	G4
Burnside Dr. (Br.Don) AB23	11	E6
Burnside Gdns. (Port.) AB12	39	E3
Burnside Gdns. AB25	23	G1
Burnside Rd. (Dyce) AB21	7	G4
Burnside Rd., Peter. AB14	32	D4
Bush, The, Peter. AB14	32	D3
Bute Way AB16	22	A1
Bydand Pl. (Br.Don) AB23	11	E4
Byron Av. AB16	13	E5
Byron Cres. AB16	12	D4
Byron Pk. AB16	13	E5
Springhill Ter.		
Byron Sq. AB16	13	E4
Byron Ter. AB16	12	D5
C		
Cadenhead Pl. AB25	14	B5
Cadenhead Rd. AB25	14	B5
Caiesdykes Cres. AB12	30	A3
Caiesdykes Dr. AB12	30	A2
Caiesdykes Rd. AB12	30	A3
Cairn Cres. (Cults) AB15	27	G3
Cairn Gdns. (Cults) AB15	27	G3
Cairn Pk. (Cults) AB15	27	G3
Cairn Rd. (Bield.) AB15	27	G3
Cairn Rd., Peter. AB14	33	E3
Cairn Wk. (Cults) AB15	27	G3
Cairnaquheen Gdns. AB15	23	F1
Cairnaquheen Pl. AB15	23	F2
Cairnaquheen Gdns.		
Cairncry Av. AB16	13	H5
Cairncry Ct. AB16	13	G5
Cairncry Cres. AB16	14	A5
Cairncry Rd. AB16	13	H5
Cairncry Ter. AB16	13	H5
Cairnfield Circle (Bucks.) AB21	13	E1
Cairnfield Cres. (Bucks.) AB21	13	E2
Cairnfield Gdns. (Bucks.) AB21	13	E2
Auchmill Rd.		
Cairnfield Pl. AB15	23	G1
Cairnfield Pl. (Bucks.) AB21	13	E2
Cairnfold Rd. (Br.Don) AB22	14	D1
Cairngorm Cres. AB12	30	B2
Cairngorm Dr. AB12	30	A2
Cairngorm Gdns. AB12	30	B2
Cairngorm Pl. AB12	30	A2
Cairngorm Rd. AB12	29	H2
Cairngrassie Circle (Port.) AB12	38	C5
Cairngrassie Dr. (Port.) AB12	38	C5
Cairnhill Dr. (Newt.), Stone. AB39	40	C4
Cairnhill Pl. (Newt.), Stone. AB39	40	C4
Cairnhill Rd. (Newt.), Stone. AB39	40	C4
Cairnhillock Pl. (Bucks.) AB21	12	B3
Newhills Av.		
Cairnie Vw., Westh. AB32	16	D3
Cairnlee Av. E. (Cults) AB15	27	G3
Cairnlee Cres. N. AB15	27	G3
Cairnlee Cres. S. (Cults) AB15	27	G3
Cairnlee Pk. (Bield.) AB15	27	F3
Cairnlee Rd. (Bield.) AB15	27	F3
Cairnlee Rd. E. (Cults) AB15	27	G2
Cairnlee Ter. (Bield.) AB15	27	F3
Cairnside (Cults) AB15	27	G3
Cairnton Ct., Westh. AB32	17	E4
Ashdale Dr.		
Cairnvale Cres. AB12	30	A2
Cairnvale Ter. AB12	30	A2
Cairnview Cres. AB16	13	H5
Cairnwell Av. AB16	13	E6
Cairnwell Dr. (Port.) AB12	38	D4
Cairnwell Dr. AB16	13	E5
Cairnwell Pl. AB16	13	E5
Caledonian Brae AB11	24	B4
Ferryhill Rd.		
Caledonian Ct. AB11	24	B4
Ferryhill Ter.		
Caledonian La. AB11	24	B4
Caledonian Pl.		
Caledonian Pl. AB11	24	B4
Callum Cres. (Kings.) AB15	18	C3
Callum Pk. (Kings.) AB15	18	C3
Callum Path (Kings.) AB15	18	C3
Callum Wynd (Kings.) AB15	18	C3
Calsayseat Rd. AB25	14	C6
Cameron Av. (Br.Don) AB23	10	D6
Cameron Dr. (Br.Don) AB23	10	D6
Cameron Pl. (Br.Don) AB23	11	E6
Cameron Rd. (Br.Don) AB23	10	D6
Cameron St. (Br.Don) AB23	11	E6
Cameron Ter. (Br.Don) AB23	10	D6
Cameron Way (Br.Don) AB23	10	D6
Cammach Circle (Port.) AB12	38	C5
Camperdown Rd. AB15	23	F1
Campsie Pl. AB15	22	D2
Campus One AB22	14	C1
Campus Three (Br.Don) AB22	14	C1
Campus Two (Br.Don) AB22	14	C1
Canal Pl. AB24	14	D6
Canal St. AB24	14	D6
Canal St. (Woodside) AB24	14	A2
Canal Ter. AB24	13	H2
Candlemakers La. AB25	24	B1
Loch St.		
Caperstown Cres. AB16	13	F4
Carden Pl. AB10	23	G3
Carden Ter. AB10	4	A3
Cardens Knowe (Br.Don) AB22	10	D6
Glashieburn Way		

Street	Map	Grid
Carlin Ter. (Dyce) AB21	7	G2
Netherview Av.		
Carlton Pl. AB15	23	F2
Carmelite La. AB11	24	C2
Wapping St.		
Carmelite St. AB11	24	C2
Wapping St.		
Carnegie Cres. AB15	23	E3
Carnegie Gdns. AB15	23	E3
Carnegies Brae AB10	24	C2
Flourmill La.		
Carnie Dr. AB25	14	A5
Carnie Gdns. AB25	14	A5
Carnie Dr.		
Carnoustie Cres. (Br.Don) AB22	10	C5
Carnoustie Gdns. (Br.Don) AB22	10	C5
Carnoustie Cres.		
Caroline Apartments AB25	24	A1
Forbes St.		
Caroline Pl. AB25	24	A1
Hutcheon St.		
Carron Pl. AB16	13	E5
Cassie Cl. (Co.Bay) AB12	30	D6
Castle St. AB11	5	D2
Castle Ter. AB11	5	E2
Castlegate AB11	24	C2
Justice St.		
Castlehill AB11	24	D1
Hanover St.		
Castleton Ct. AB16	13	G6
Castleton Dr.		
Castleton Cres. AB16	13	G6
Castleton Dr. AB16	13	G6
Castleton La. AB16	13	G6
Castleton Cres.		
Castleton Pk. AB16	13	G6
Castleton Cres.		
Castleton Way AB16	13	G6
Castleton Cres.		
Catherine St. AB25	4	C1
Catto Cres. (Co.Bay) AB12	31	E6
Catto Wk. (Co.Bay) AB12	31	E6
Cattofield Gdns. AB25	14	B5
Cattofield Pl. AB25	14	B5
Cattofield Ter. AB25	14	B5
Causewayend AB25	14	D6
Cava AB15	22	A1
Cedar Pl. AB25	14	B6
Centre Point (Br.Don) AB23	11	E4
Chanonry AB24	14	D3
Chapel Ct. AB11	24	D2
Justice St.		
Chapel Rd. (Newt.), Stone. AB39	41	E4
Chapel St. AB10	4	B2
Chapman Pl. AB16	13	E3
Provost Rust Dr.		
Chapman Wk. AB16	13	E3
Provost Rust Dr.		
Chapman Wk. AB16	13	E3
Howes Cres.		
Charles Pl. AB25	14	D6
Charles St.		
Charles St. AB25	14	D6
Charleston Av. (Co. Bay) AB12	37	E2
Charleston Circle (Co. Bay) AB12	37	E2
Charleston Cres. (Co. Bay) AB12	37	E1
Charleston Dr. (Co. Bay) AB12	36	D2
Charleston Gdns. (Co. Bay) AB12	37	E1
Charleston Gro. (Co. Bay) AB12	36	D1
Charleston Pl. (Co. Bay) AB12	36	D2
Charleston Rd. (Co. Bay) AB12	30	C6
Charleston Wk. (Co. Bay) AB12	37	E1
Charleston Way (Co. Bay) AB12	37	E1
Charlotte Gdns. AB25	4	C1
Charlotte Pl. AB25	4	C1
Charlotte St. AB25	4	C1
Chattan Pl. AB10	23	H4
Cherry Rd. AB16	13	H5
Chestnut Row AB25	14	B6
Cheyne Rd. AB24	15	E3
Church La. (Bucks.) AB21	12	B1
Inverurie Rd.		
Church St. AB11	5	E2
Church St. (Woodside) AB24	14	A3
Church Wk. AB24	14	D4
High St.		
Churchill Rd. AB23	11	F6
Claremont Gdns. AB10	23	H4
Claremont Gro. AB10	23	H4
Claremont Pl. AB10	23	H4
Claremont St. AB10	23	H4
Clarence St. AB11	5	E2
Clarke St. AB16	13	G3
Clarks La. AB24	15	E3
Clashbog Pl. (Bucks.) AB21	12	B2
Clashfarquhar Cres. (Port.) AB12	38	C3
Clashieknowe (Br.Don) AB22	10	D6
Scotstown Rd.		
Clashnettie Pl. (Dyce) AB21	7	G3
Clashrodney Av. (Co.Bay) AB12	37	F1
Clashrodney Rd. (Co.Bay) AB12	37	F1
Clashrodney Wk. (Co.Bay) AB12	37	F1
Clashrodney Way (Co.Bay) AB12	37	F1
Claymore Av. (Port.) AB12	39	E2
Claymore Av. (Br.Don) AB23	11	G4
Claymore Dr. (Br.Don) AB23	11	G4
Clerk Maxwell Cres. AB12	29	H4
Cliff Pk. (Cults) AB15	28	B2
Cliff Vw. (Newt.), Stone. AB39	40	D4
Clifton Ct. AB24	14	B3
Great Northern Rd.		
Clifton La. AB24	14	B4
Clifton Pl. AB24	14	B4
Clifton Rd. AB24	13	H3
Cloghill Pl. AB16	22	B1
Sheddocksley Dr.		
Clova Cres. (Kings.) AB15	18	C4
Clova Pk. (Kings.) AB15	18	C4
Clover Meadow, Westh. AB32	16	B4
Cloverdale Ct. (Bucks.) AB21	12	B1
Sclattie Pk.		
Cloverfield Ct. (Bucks.) AB21	12	A1
Cloverfield Gdns. (Bucks.) AB21	12	B1
Cloverfield Pl. (Bucks.) AB21	12	A1
Cloverhill Rd. (Br.Don) AB22	10	C6
Cloverhill Rd. (Br.Don) AB23	11	E6
Clunie Pl. AB16	13	E5
Clyde St. AB11	5	E3
Coldstone Av. (Kings.) AB15	18	C4
Coll Wk. AB16	22	A1
College Bounds AB24	14	D4
College St. AB11	5	C3
Collieston Av. (Br.Don) AB22	10	C4
Collieston Circle (Br.Don) AB22	10	C5
Collieston Cres. (Br.Don) AB22	10	D4
Collieston Dr. (Br.Don) AB22	10	D5
Collieston Path (Br.Don) AB22	10	C4
Collieston Pl. (Br.Don) AB22	10	C5
Collieston Rd. (Br.Don) AB22	10	C5
Collieston St. (Br.Don) AB22	10	D5
Collieston Way (Br.Don) AB22	10	D4
Colonsay Cres. AB16	22	A1
Colsea Rd. (Co.Bay) AB12	37	G1
Colsea Sq. (Co.Bay) AB12	37	G1
Colsea Rd.		
Colsea Ter. (Co.Bay) AB12	37	G1
Colthill Circle, Mill. AB13	26	B5
Colthill Cres., Mill. AB13	26	B4
Colthill Dr., Mill. AB13	26	B5
Colthill Rd., Mill. AB13	26	B4
Colville Pl. AB24	15	E6
Commerce St. AB11	5	E2
Commercial Quay AB11	5	E3
Concert Ct. AB10	24	C2
Broad St.		
Concraig Gdns. (Kings.) AB15	19	E3
Concraig Pl. (Kings.) AB15	19	E3
Conference Way (Br.Don) AB23	11	F5
Coningham Gdns. AB24	14	C3
Coningham Rd. AB24	14	C3
Coningham Ter. AB24	14	C3
Constitution Ct. AB24	24	D1
Constitution St.		
Constitution La. AB24	24	D1
Wales St.		
Constitution St. AB24	5	E1
Contlaw Brae, Mill. AB13	26	B5
Contlaw Pl., Mill. AB13	26	B5
Contlaw Rd., Mill. AB13	26	A4
Cookston Rd. (Port.) AB12	38	D2
Corby Ter. (Dyce) AB21	7	G3
Cordyce Vw. (Dyce) AB21	7	E3
Cormorant Brae (Co. Bay) AB12	30	C5
Corndavon Ter. AB16	13	F6
Cornhill Ct. AB16	13	H5
Cornhill Dr. AB16	13	H5
Cornhill Gdns. AB16	13	H5
Cornhill Rd. AB25	13	H6
Cornhill Shopping Arc. AB16	13	G5
Cornhill Dr.		
Cornhill Sq. AB16	14	A5
Ash-hill Rd.		
Cornhill Ter. AB16	13	H5
Cornhill Way AB16	13	H6
Cornyhaugh Rd., Peter. AB14	32	C2
Coronation Ct., Peter. AB14	33	E3
Coronation Rd.		
Coronation Rd., Peter. AB14	33	E3
Correction Wynd AB10	24	C2
Schoolhill		
Corrennie Circle (Dyce) AB21	7	F1
Corse Av. (Kings.) AB15	18	C3
Corse Gdns. (Kings.) AB15	18	D3
Corse Wynd (Kings.) AB15	18	D3
Corsehill Gdns. (Br.Don) AB22	14	C1
Corthan Cres. AB12	30	B1
Corthan Dr. AB12	30	B1
Corthan Pl. AB12	30	B1
Corunna Rd. AB23	15	F1
Cothal Vw. AB21	7	E1
Cottage Brae AB10	23	H4
Cotton St. AB11	5	E1
Cottown of Balgownie AB23	15	E1
Coull Gdns. (Kings.) AB15	18	C4
Coull Gdns. (Kings.) AB15	14	D1
Coull Grn. (Kings.) AB15	18	C4
Countesswells Av. AB15	22	B5
Countesswells Cres. AB15	22	B5
Countesswells Pl. AB15	22	C5
Countesswells Rd. AB15	22	D6
Countesswells Ter. AB15	22	C5
Courtyard, The (Cults) AB15	28	A3
Millden Rd.		
Cove Circle (Co.Bay) AB12	37	F1
Cove Cl. (Co.Bay) AB12	37	G1
Cove Cres. (Co.Bay) AB12	37	F2
Cove Gdns. (Co.Bay) AB12	37	F1
Cove Path (Co.Bay) AB12	37	G1
Cove Pl. (Co. Bay) AB12	37	G1
Cove Rd. (Co.Bay) AB12	37	F1
Cove Wk. (Co.Bay) AB12	37	F1
Cove Way (Co.Bay) AB12	37	F1
Cove Wynd (Co.Bay) AB12	37	F1
Covenanters Dr. AB12	30	B1
Covenanters Row AB12	30	A1
Cowan Pl. AB24	14	B2
Alexander Dr.		
Craibstone Av. (Bucks.) AB21	7	F6
Craibstone La. AB11	24	B4
Bon Accord St.		
Craig Gdns. (Cults) AB15	27	G3
Craig Pl. AB11	24	C4
Menzies Rd.		
Craig Pl. (Newt.), Stone. AB39	41	E4
Craigendarroch Av. AB16	13	F5
Craigendarroch Pl. AB16	13	F5
Craighaar Gables (Bucks.) AB21	8	C5
Stoneywood Rd.		
Craighead Av. (Port.) AB12	38	C3
Craighill Caravan Pk. (Bridge of Dee) AB12	30	A5
Craighill Ter. (Co.Bay) AB12	37	G1
Spark Ter.		
Craigie Loanings AB25	4	A2
Craigie Pk. AB25	4	A2
Craigie Pk. Pl. AB25	4	A2
Craigie St. AB25	4	C1
Craigiebuckler Av. AB15	22	C4
Craigiebuckler Dr. AB15	22	C4
Craigiebuckler Pl. AB15	22	C4
Craigiebuckler Ter. AB15	22	C4
Craigieburn Pk. AB15	22	D5
Craigielea Av. AB15	23	F5
Craigielea Gdns. AB15	23	E5
Craigielea Ms. AB15	23	E5
Craigievar Ct. AB10	29	G2
Craigievar Cres. AB10	29	F2
Craigievar Gdns. AB10	29	F2
Craigievar Pl. AB10	29	F1
Craigievar Rd. AB10	29	G2
Craigievar Ter. AB10	29	G2
Craigmarn Rd. (Port.) AB12	39	F4
Craigmaroinn Gdns. AB12	30	D5

Street	Map	Grid
Craignook Rd. (Dyce) AB21	7	G2
Balloch Way		
Craigpark AB18	30	D2
Craigshaw Cres. AB12	30	C1
Craigshaw Dr. AB12	30	C2
Craigshaw Pl. AB12	30	C1
Craigshaw Rd. AB12	30	C1
Craigshaw St. AB12	30	C1
Craigston Gdns., Westh. AB32	17	F3
Craigston Pl., Westh. AB32	17	F3
Craigston Rd., Westh. AB32	17	F3
Craigton Av. AB15	23	E6
Craigton Ct. AB15	23	F6
Craigton Cres., Peter. AB14	32	D3
Craigton Dr., Peter. AB14	32	D3
Craigton Gro., Peter. AB14	32	D3
Craigton Pk. AB15	23	E6
Craigton Rd. AB15	23	E6
Craigton Ter. AB15	23	E6
Craigton Ter., Peter. AB14	32	D3
Cranford Pl. AB10	23	F6
Cranford Rd. AB10	23	F6
Cranford Ter. AB10	23	F6
Cranhill Brae (Newt.), Stone. AB39	41	E4
Cranhill Pl. (Newt.), Stone. AB39	41	E3
Crathie Gdns. W. AB10	24	A6
Crathie Ter. AB10	23	H6
Crawpeel Rd. (Altens Ind. Est.) AB12	30	D4
Crawton Ness AB12	30	D5
Creel Av. (Co. Bay) AB12	37	E2
Creel Ct. (Co. Bay) AB12	37	E2
Creel Dr. (Co. Bay) AB12	37	F1
Creel Gdns. (Co. Bay) AB12	37	F1
Creel Pl. (Co. Bay) AB12	37	F2
Creel Rd. (Co. Bay) AB12	37	E2
Creel Wk. (Co. Bay) AB12	37	F1
Creel Wynd (Co. Bay) AB12	37	F2
Crimon Pl. AB10	4	C2
Croft Pl. AB16	22	C1
Croft Rd. AB16	22	C1
Croft Ter. AB16	13	E6
Crollshillock Pl. (Newt.), Stone. AB39	40	D4
Cromar Gdns. (Kings.) AB15	18	D4
Crombie Acres, Westh. AB32	16	B4
Crombie Circle, Peter. AB14	32	C2
Crombie Circle, Westh. AB32	16	C4
Crombie Cl., Westh. AB32	16	C4
Crombie Dr., Westh. AB32	16	B4
Crombie Pl. AB11	24	D4
Crombie Pl., Westh. AB32	16	B4
Crombie Acres		
Crombie Rd. AB11	24	D4
Crombie Rd., Westh. AB32	16	B4
Crombie Wynd, Westh. AB32	16	B4
Cromwell Ct. AB15	23	G4
Forbesfield Rd.		
Cromwell Gdns. AB15	23	F4
Cromwell Rd. AB15	23	F4
Crooked La. AB25	5	C1
Crookfold Gdns. (Br.Don) AB23	11	E6
Crookfold Pl. (Br.Don) AB23	11	E6
Crossgates (Bucks.) AB21	8	C6
Crown Cres., Peter. AB14	33	E2
Crown La. AB11	24	B3
Crown Ter.		
Crown Pl., Peter. AB14	33	E2
Crown St. AB11	5	C3
Crown Ter. AB11	5	C3
Crown Ter., Peter. AB14	33	E3
Cruden Cres. AB16	12	D4
Cruden Pk. AB16	12	D4
Cruden Pl. AB16	12	D4
Cruickshank Ct., Westh. AB32	16	B5
Cruickshank Cres. AB32	30	A3
Cruickshank Cres. (Bucks.) AB21	12	B2
Culter Den, Peter. AB14	32	C3
Culter Ho. Rd., Mill. AB13	26	A5
Cults Av. (Cults) AB15	27	H2
Cults Business Pk. (Cults) AB15	28	B2
Station Rd.		
Cults Ct. (Cults) AB15	28	A3
Cults Gdns. (Cults) AB15	28	A2
Cummings Pk. Circle AB16	13	G4
Cummings Pk. Cres. AB16	13	F4
Cummings Pk. Dr. AB16	13	F4
Cummings Pk. Rd. AB16	13	G3
Cummings Pk. Ter. AB16	13	F4
Cuparstone Ct. AB10	24	A3
Cuparstone Row		
Cuparstone La. AB10	24	A3
Cuparstone Row		
Cuparstone Row AB10	4	B3
Cypress Av. (Br.Don) AB23	10	D2
Cypress Gro. (Br.Don) AB23	10	D2
Cypress Wk. (Br.Don) AB23	10	D2

D

Street	Map	Grid
Dalmaik Cres., Peter. AB14	32	D2
Dalmaik Ter., Peter. AB14	32	D2
Dalmuinzie Rd. (Bield.) AB15	27	H3
Dancing Cairns Cres. AB16	13	E3
Dancing Cairns Pl. AB16	13	E2
Danestone Circle AB16	13	G3
Danestone Pl. (Br.Don) AB23	15	E1
Danestone Ter. (Br.Don) AB23	15	E1
Darroch Pk. (Cults) AB15	27	H3
Davan Pk. (Br.Don) AB22	14	D1
Davidson Dr. AB16	12	D3
Davidson Gdns. AB16	12	D4
Davidson Ho. AB15	22	B3
Hazlehead Rd.		
Davidson Pl. AB16	12	D4
Dawson Cl., Westh. AB32	16	B4
Old Skene Rd.		
Dawson Dr., Westh. AB32	16	B4
Old Skene Rd.		
Dawson Wynd, Westh. AB32	16	B4
Old Skene Rd.		
Dean Gdns., Westh. AB32	17	F4
Deansloch Cres. AB16	13	E4
Deansloch Pl. AB16	13	E4
Deansloch Ter. AB16	13	E4
Dee Pl. AB11	5	C3
Dee St. AB11	4	C3
Deemount Av. AB11	24	B5
Deemount Gdns. AB11	24	B5
Deemount Rd. AB11	24	B5
Deemount Ter. AB11	24	B5
Deer Rd. (Woodside) AB24	14	A3
Deeside Av. AB15	29	E1
Deeside Cres. AB15	29	E1
Deeside Dr. AB15	29	E1
Deeside Gdns. AB15	29	E1
Deeside Pk. AB15	29	E1
Deeside Pl. AB15	29	E1
Deeside Ter. AB15	29	E1
Deevale Cres. AB12	30	A2
Deevale Gdns. AB12	30	A2
Deevale Rd. AB12	30	A2
Deevale Ter. AB12	30	A2
Deeview Rd. S. (Cults) AB15	28	A3
Delgaty La. (Dyce) AB21	7	F2
Belmuir Gdns.		
Dempsey Ter. AB24	14	C3
Den, The (Cults) AB15	28	B3
Den of Cults (Cults) AB15	28	B2
Denburn Ct. AB25	24	B1
Gilcomston Pk.		
Denburn Rd. AB11	4	C2
Denburn Rd. AB25	4	C2
Denmore Ct. (Br.Don) AB23	11	E3
Dubford Rd.		
Denmore Gdns. (Br.Don) AB22	14	D1
Denmore Ind. Est. (Br.Don) AB23	11	E3
Denmore Pl. (Br.Don) AB23	11	E3
Denmore Rd. (Br.Don) AB23	11	E3
Denseat Ct. AB15	22	A2
Queens Den		
Denseat Rd. AB15	22	A2
Denwood AB15	22	B2
Derbeth Cres. AB16	22	A1
Derbeth Pk. (Kings.) AB15	18	D2
Derbeth Pl. (Kings.) AB15	18	D2
Derry Av. AB16	13	F6
Derry Pl. AB16	13	F6
Desswood Pl. AB15	23	G3
Desswood Pl. AB15	23	G3
Devanha Cres. AB11	24	B4
Devanha Gdns. AB11	24	B4
Devanha Gdns. E. AB11	24	B4
Devanha Gdns. S. AB11	24	B5
Devanha Gdns. W. AB11	24	B4
Devanha La. AB11	24	B4
Devanha Gdns.		
Devanha Ter. AB11	24	B4
Devenick Dr. (Port.) AB12	39	E2
Devenick Pl. AB10	29	F2
Deveron Rd. AB16	12	D5
Devonshire Rd. AB10	23	G4
Diamond La. AB10	24	B2
Diamond St.		
Diamond Pl. AB10	24	B2
Union Ter.		
Diamond St. AB10	4	C2
Dickson Ter. AB16	12	D5
Dill Pl. AB24	14	B2
Dill Rd. AB24	14	B2
Dinbaith Pl. AB16	22	A1
Derbeth Cres.		
Dock St. E. AB11	25	E3
Blaikies Quay		
Dock St. W. AB11	25	E3
Blaikies Quay		
Dominies Ct. AB16	13	H4
Dominies Rd. AB16	13	H4
Don Ct. (Woodside) AB24	13	H2
Don Gdns. (Woodside) AB24	14	A2
Don Pl. (Dyce) AB21	7	F3
Don Pl. AB24	14	B3
Don St. (Old Aberdeen) AB24	14	D3
Don St. (Woodside) AB24	14	B3
Don Ter. (Woodside) AB24	14	A2
Donald Pl. AB25	4	B1
Donbank Ter. AB24	14	B2
Donmouth Ct. (Br.Don) AB23	15	F1
Donmouth Cres. (Br.Don) AB23	15	F1
Donmouth Gdns. (Br.Don) AB23	15	F1
Donmouth Rd. (Br.Don) AB23	15	F2
Donmouth Ter. (Br.Don) AB23	15	F1
Donside Ct. AB24	14	B2
Auchinleck Rd.		
Donview Ho. AB24	15	F3
Donview Pl. AB24	14	B2
Donview Rd. AB24	14	A2
Doolie Ness AB12	30	D5
Douglas La. AB24	14	D4
High St.		
Douglas Pl. AB24	14	D4
High St.		
Downies Brae AB11	24	D5
Downies Pl. AB11	25	E5
Downies Rd. (Port.) AB12	39	E4
Drinnies Cres. (Dyce) AB21	7	G2
Drumthwacket Dr. (Port.) AB12	38	C5
Dubford Av. (Br.Don) AB23	10	D3
Dubford Cres. (Br.Don) AB23	10	D3
Dubford Gdns. (Br.Don) AB23	10	D2
Dubford Gro. (Br.Don) AB23	10	D2
Dubford Pk. (Br.Don) AB23	10	D4
Dubford Pl. (Br.Don) AB23	10	D3
Dubford Ri. (Br.Don) AB23	10	D2
Dubford Rd. (Br.Don) AB23	10	D3
Dubford Ter. (Br.Don) AB23	10	D3
Dubford Wk. (Br.Don) AB23	10	D2
Duff St. AB24	5	E1
Dugald Baird Ct. AB12	30	A4
Clerk Maxwell Cres.		
Dugald Baird Sq. AB12	30	A4
Clerk Maxwell Cres.		
Dulnain Rd. AB16	12	D6
Dumgoyne Pl. AB15	22	D2
Dunbar St. AB24	14	D4
Dunbennan Rd. (Dyce) AB21	7	G2
Duncans Pl. AB24	14	D4
High St.		
Dunecht Gdns., Westh. AB32	16	C4
Dunecht Rd., Westh. AB32	16	C4
Dunlin Ct. (Newt.), Stone. AB39	41	E3
Dunlin Cres. (Co.Bay) AB12	30	D6
Dunlin Rd. (Co.Bay) AB12	30	C6
Dunmail Av. (Cults) AB15	28	A3
Dunnyfell Rd. (Muchalls), Stone. AB39	40	B6
Dunvegan Av. (Port.) AB12	38	D3
Dunvegan Cres. (Port.) AB12	38	D3
Dunvegan Pl. (Port.) AB12	38	D3
Duthie Ct. AB10	23	F5
Duthie Ter.		
Duthie Pl. AB10	23	F6
Duthie Ter. AB10	23	F6
Dyce Dr. (Dyce) AB21	6	D6
Dyce Ind. Est. (Dyce) AB21	7	G6
Dyce Shopping Cen. (Dyce) AB21	7	H3

Name	Page	Grid
Dykeside Way (Bucks.) AB21	12	B3
Newhills Av.		
E		
Earls Ct. Gdns. AB15	23	E3
Earlspark Av. (Bield.) AB15	27	F2
Earlspark Circle (Bield.) AB15	27	F2
Earlspark Cres. (Bield.) AB15	27	F2
Earlspark Dr. (Bield.) AB15	27	F3
Earlspark Gdns. (Bield.) AB15	27	F2
Earlspark Rd. (Bield.) AB15	27	F3
Earlspark Way (Bield.) AB15	27	G2
Earlspark Av.		
Earlswells Dr. (Cults) AB15	27	G3
Earlswells Pl. (Cults) AB15	27	G3
Earlswells Rd. (Cults) AB15	27	G3
Earlswells Vw. (Cults) AB15	27	G2
Earlswells Wk. (Cults) AB15	27	G3
Earn's Heugh Av. (Co.Bay) AB12	37	F1
Earn's Heugh Circle (Co.Bay) AB12	37	F1
Earn's Heugh Cres. (Co.Bay) AB12	37	F1
Earn's Heugh Pl. (Co.Bay) AB12	30	D6
Earn's Heugh Rd. AB12	30	D5
Earn's Heugh Vw. (Co.Bay) AB12	30	D6
Earn's Heugh Wk. (Co.Bay) AB12	30	D6
Earn's Heugh Way (Co.Bay) AB12	37	F1
Earnsheugh Rd. (Port.) AB12	39	H2
Earnsheugh Ter. (Port.) AB12	39	H2
East Craibstone St. AB11	24	B4
Bon Accord St.		
East Grn. AB11	24	C2
Market St.		
East Main Av. AB16	13	F6
East N. St. AB24	5	D1
East Tullos Ind. Est. AB12	25	E6
Easter Ct. (Port.) AB12	38	D5
Easter Dr. (Port.) AB12	38	D5
Easter Pl. (Port.) AB12	38	D5
Eastside Av., Westh. AB32	17	E4
Eastside Dr., Westh. AB32	17	E3
Eastside Grn., Westh. AB32	17	E3
Eastsyde Pl. (Port.) AB12	38	C5
Eday Cres. AB15	22	B1
Eday Dr. AB15	22	B1
Eday Gdns. AB15	22	A2
Eday Rd. AB15	22	C2
Eday Sq. AB15	22	B1
Eday Wk. AB15	22	B2
Eden Pl. AB25	4	B1
Edgehill Rd. AB15	23	E2
Edgehill Ter. AB15	23	E2
Edmond Gdns. (Kings.) AB15	18	D5
Eldenside, Peter. AB14	32	C2
Elder Pl. AB25	14	A5
Ellerslie Rd. (Bucks.) AB21	8	C6
Ellon Rd. (Br.Don) AB23	11	F6
Elm Pl. AB25	14	B6
Elmbank Rd. AB24	14	D6
Elmbank Ter. AB24	14	C5
Elmfield Av. AB24	14	C5
Elmfield Pl. AB24	14	C5
Elmfield Ter. AB24	14	C5
Elphinstone Ct. AB24	14	B2
Auchinleck Cres.		
Elphinstone Rd. AB24	14	D4
Elrick Circle (Br.Don) AB22	10	C6
Elsick Pl. (Newt.), Stone. AB39	40	D4
Endrick Pl. AB15	22	D1
Enterprise Dr., Westh. AB32	16	D6
Eriskay Dr. AB16	21	H1
Errol Pl. AB24	15	E6
Errol St. AB24	15	E6
Erskine St. AB24	14	C5
Esk Pl. AB16	13	E5
Esplanade AB24	25	E2
Esslemont Av. AB25	4	A1
Exchange La. AB11	24	C2
Exchange St.		
Exchange St. AB11	5	D2
Exchequer Row AB11	24	C2
Shiprow		
Exhibition Av. (Br.Don) AB23	11	F6
Exploration Dr. (Br.Don) AB23	11	F5
F		
Fairies Knowe (Bucks.) AB21	12	B2
Fairley Den (Bucks.) AB21	12	B1
Sclattie Pk.		
Fairley Rd. (Kings.) AB15	18	D5
Fairlie St. AB16	13	G3
Fairview Av. (Dane.) AB22	9	H6
Fairview Brae (Dane.) AB22	13	H1
Fairview Circle (Dane.) AB22	9	G6
Fairview Cres. (Dane.) AB22	9	H6
Fairview Dr. (Dane.) AB22	13	H1
Fairview Gdns. (Dane.) AB22	9	G6
Fairview Gra. (Br.Don) AB22	9	G6
Fairview Gro. (Dane.) AB22	9	H6
Fairview Manor (Dane.) AB22	13	H1
Fairview Par. (Dane.) AB22	9	H6
Fairview Pk. (Dane.) AB22	9	H6
Fairview Pl. (Dane.) AB22	9	H6
Fairview Rd. (Dane.) AB22	9	G6
Fairview St. (Dane.) AB22	9	H6
Fairview Ter. (Dane.) AB22	9	G6
Fairview Wk. (Dane.) AB22	10	A6
Fairview Way (Dane.) AB22	9	H6
Fairview Wynd (Dane.) AB22	10	A6
Falkland Av. (Co.Bay) AB12	31	E6
Fallow Rd., Westh. AB32	16	B4
Fara Cl. AB15	21	H1
Farburn Ind. Est. (Dyce) AB21	7	G5
Farburn Ter. (Dyce) AB21	7	F4
Fare Pk. Circle, Westh. AB32	16	D3
Fare Pk. Cres., Westh. AB32	17	E3
Fare Pk. Dr., Westh. AB32	16	D4
Fare Pk. Gdns., Westh. AB32	16	D4
Farmers Hall La. AB25	4	B1
Farquhar Av. AB11	25	E5
Farquhar Brae AB11	25	E5
Farquhar Rd. AB11	24	D6
Farrier La. AB24	24	C1
Mealmarket St.		
Fassiefern Av. (Br.Don) AB23	11	E4
Faulds Cres. AB12	30	A1
Faulds Gate AB12	30	A2
Faulds Row AB12	30	B2
Faulds Wynd AB12	30	B1
Fergus Pl. (Dyce) AB21	7	F2
Ferguson Ct. (Bucks.) AB21	12	D1
Oldmeldrum Rd.		
Fern Dr. (Port.) AB12	38	D4
Fern Pl. (Port.) AB12	38	D4
Fernhill Dr. AB16	13	E6
Fernhill Pl. AB16	22	B1
Fernhill Rd. AB16	22	B1
Fernie Brae AB11	24	D6
Fernielea Cres. AB15	22	C2
Fernielea Pl. AB15	22	C2
Fernielea Rd. AB15	22	C2
Ferrier Cres. AB24	14	B3
Ferrier Gdns. AB24	14	B3
Ferry Pl. AB11	25	E3
Ferryhill Gdns. AB11	24	B4
Ferryhill La. AB11	24	B4
Ferryhill Pl. AB11	24	B4
Ferryhill Rd. AB11	24	B4
Ferryhill Ter. AB11	24	B4
Fetach Wk. (Dyce) AB21	7	F2
Fifehill Pk. AB21	7	G3
Findhorn Pl. AB16	12	D6
Findon Ness AB12	31	E5
Findon Pl. (Port.) AB12	39	H1
Findon Rd. (Port.) AB12	39	G1
Finnan Brae AB11	25	F4
Finnan Pl. AB11	25	F4
Finnan Brae		
Fintray Rd. AB15	22	C4
Firhill Pl. AB24	14	D5
Spital Wk.		
Firhill Rd. AB24	14	D5
Fish St. AB11	5	E2
Fittick Pl. (Co.Bay) AB12	31	E6
Flourmill La. AB10	5	D2
Fonthill Gdns. E. AB11	24	A5
Fonthill Gdns. W. AB11	24	A4
Fonthill Rd. AB11	24	A4
Fonthill Ter. AB11	24	A4
Forbes St. AB25	4	B1
Forbesfield La. AB15	23	G4
Forbesfield Rd. AB15	23	G4
Forehill La. (Br.Don) AB22	10	D6
Glashieburn Way		
Forest Av. AB15	23	G4
Forest Av. La. AB15	23	G4
Forest Rd. AB15	23	F2
Foresterhill Ct. AB25	23	G1
Foresters Av. (Bucks.) AB21	8	C5
Forestgait AB15	23	F2
Formartine Rd. AB24	14	B3
Forresterhill Rd. AB16	13	G5
Forresterhill Rd. AB25	13	H6
Forrit Brae (Bucks.) AB21	8	A6
Forties Rd. (Dyce) AB21	6	C4
Forvie Av. (Br.Don) AB22	10	C5
Forvie Circle (Br.Don) AB22	10	C4
Forvie Cl. (Br.Don) AB22	10	C4
Forvie Cres. (Br.Don) AB22	10	C5
Forvie La. (Br.Don) AB22	10	C5
Forvie Pk. AB22	10	C5
Jesmond Rd.		
Forvie Path (Br.Don) AB22	10	C5
Forvie Pl. (Br.Don) AB22	10	C5
Forvie Rd. (Br.Don) AB22	10	C4
Forvie St. (Br.Don) AB22	10	C4
Forvie Ter. (Br.Don) AB22	10	C5
Forvie Way (Br.Don) AB22	10	C5
Fountainhall Rd. AB15	23	G2
Fountville Ct. AB24	14	A3
Summer St.		
Foveran Path (Br.Don) AB22	10	C5
Foveran Ri. (Br.Don) AB22	10	B4
Foveran St. (Br.Don) AB22	10	B4
Foveran Way (Br.Don) AB22	10	B5
Fowler Av. AB16	13	F3
Fowlershill Gdns. (Br.Don) AB22	14	D1
Fraser Ct. AB25	14	D6
Fraser Dr., Westh. AB32	16	C5
Fraser Pl. AB25	14	C6
Fraser Rd. AB25	14	C6
Fraser St. AB25	14	C6
Fraserfield Gdns. (Br.Don) AB23	11	E1
Frederick St. AB24	5	D1
Friarsfield Rd. (Cults) AB15	28	A2
Friendship Ter. AB10	23	H4
Ashley Rd.		
Froghall Av. AB24	14	D6
Froghall Gdns. AB24	14	D6
Froghall Pl. AB24	14	D5
Froghall Rd. AB24	14	D6
Froghall Ter. AB24	14	D6
Froghall Vw. AB24	14	D5
Fullerton Ct. AB24	13	G2
Fulmar Ct. (Newt.), Stone. AB39	41	E3
G		
Gadie Cres. AB16	13	E5
Gaelic La. AB10	24	B2
Belmont St.		
Gairn Circle AB10	24	A5
Gairn Ct. AB10	24	A5
Gairn Cres. AB10	24	A5
Gairn Rd. AB10	24	A5
Gairn Ter. AB10	24	A5
Gairnshiel Av. AB16	13	F5
Gairnshiel Pl. AB16	13	F5
Gairsay Dr. AB15	22	B1
Gairsay Rd. AB15	22	B1
Gairsay Sq. AB15	22	B1
Gaitside Cres. AB10	29	E2
Gaitside Dr. AB10	29	E2
Gaitside Pl. AB10	29	F1
Gaitside Rd. AB10	29	E2
Gaitside Ter. AB10	29	E2
Gallowgate AB10	5	D1
Gallowgate AB25	5	D1
Gallowhill Ter. (Dyce) AB21	7	H2
Garden City AB15	22	D1
Garden Ct. AB23	11	E4
Garden Rd. (Cults) AB15	27	H2
Gardner Cres. AB12	29	H3
Gardner Dr. AB12	29	H3
Gardner Pl. AB12	29	H3
Gardner Rd. AB12	29	H2
Gardner Wk. AB12	30	A3
Garmaddie La. (Dyce) AB21	7	F2
Sluie Dr.		
Garthdee Cres. AB10	29	G1
Garthdee Dr. AB10	29	G1
Garthdee Gdns. AB10	29	G1
Garthdee Rd. AB10	29	G2
Garthdee Rd. (Cults) AB15	29	F2
Garthdee Ter. AB10	29	G1
Garvock Wynd AB11	5	E2

George St. AB25	14	D6
Gerrard St. AB25	5	C1
Gilbert Rd. (Bucks.) AB21	12	C1
Gilcomston Ct. AB10	24	A2
Kidd St.		
Gilcomston Land AB10	24	A2
Kidd St.		
Gilcomston Pk. AB25	4	B2
Gilcomston Steps AB25	4	B1
Gilcomston Ter. AB25	24	A1
Farmers Hall La.		
Gillahill Pl. AB16	13	F6
Gillahill Rd. AB16	13	F6
Gillespie Cres. AB25	14	A5
Gillespie Pl. AB25	14	A5
Girdleness Rd. AB11	25	E5
Girdleness Ter. AB11	24	D6
Girdlestone Pl. AB11	25	E5
Gladstone Pl. AB10	23	G3
Gladstone Pl. (Dyce) AB21	7	F3
Gladstone Pl. (Woodside) AB24	14	A2
Glascairn Av. (Port.) AB12	38	D3
Glascairn Pl. (Port.) AB12	38	D3
Glashieburn Av. (Br.Don) AB22	10	C4
Glashieburn Way (Br.Don) AB22	10	D6
Glebe Ct. (Port.) AB12	39	E3
Glen Av. (Dyce) AB21	7	F3
Glen Dr. (Dyce) AB21	7	F3
Glen Gdns. (Dyce) AB21	7	F3
Glen Rd. (Dyce) AB21	7	F3
Glenbervie Rd. AB11	24	D4
Glendale Ms. AB11	24	A3
Union Glen		
Glendee Ter. (Cults) AB15	28	B2
Gleneagles Av. (Br.Don) AB22	10	C5
Gleneagles Dr. (Br.Don) AB22	10	C5
Gleneagles Gdns. (Br.Don) AB22	10	C5
Gleneagles Wk. (Br.Don) AB22	10	C5
Gleneagles Av.		
Glenhome Av. (Dyce) AB21	7	F4
Glenhome Ct. (Dyce) AB21	7	G3
Glenhome Cres. (Dyce) AB21	7	F4
Glenhome Gdns. (Dyce) AB21	7	F4
Glenhome Ter. (Dyce) AB21	7	F4
Glenhome Wk. (Dyce) AB21	7	G4
Glentanar Cres. (Dyce) AB21	7	G2
Golden Sq. AB10	4	C2
Golf Rd. (Bield.) AB15	27	G4
Golf Rd. AB24	15	F5
Golfview Rd. (Bield.) AB15	27	G4
Goodhope Rd. (Bucks.) AB21	13	E1
Gordon Av. (Br.Don) AB23	11	E6
Gordon Barracks (Br.Don) AB23	11	F6
Gordon Cl., Westh. AB32	16	D4
Gordon Gdns., Westh. AB32	17	E4
Gordon La. AB15	23	E6
Gordon Lennox Cres. AB23	11	E4
Gordon Pl. (Br.Don) AB23	11	E6
Gordon Rd. AB15	23	E6
Gordon Rd. (Br.Don) AB23	11	E6
Gordon St. AB11	4	C3
Gordon Ter. AB15	23	E6
Gordon Ter. (Dyce) AB21	7	F3
Gordondale Ct. AB15	23	F2
Gordondale Rd. AB15	23	G1
Gordon's Mills Cres. AB24	14	B2
Gordon's Mills Pl. AB24	14	B2
Gordon's Mills Rd. AB24	14	A2
Gorse Circle (Port.) AB12	38	D5
Gort Rd. AB24	14	B2
Gort Ter. AB24	14	B2
Auchinleck Rd.		
Goval Ter. (Dyce) AB21	7	G3
Gowanbrae Rd. (Bield.) AB15	27	F4
Graeme Av. (Dyce) AB21	7	F3
Grampian Ct. AB11	25	F5
Balnagask Circle		
Grampian Gdns. (Dyce) AB21	7	H4
Grampian La. AB11	24	D4
Grampian Pl. AB11	24	C5
Grampian Rd. AB11	24	D5
Grandholm Br. (Private) AB22	14	A2
Grandholm Ct. AB24	14	B2
Montgomery Rd.		
Grandholm St. AB24	14	A3
Grange, The, Westh. AB32	16	C4
Granitehill Pl. AB16	13	G5
Granitehill Rd. AB16	13	F3
Granitehill Ter. (Persley) AB22	13	F1
Grant Cl., Westh. AB32	17	E4
Granton Pl. AB10	4	A3
Grants Pl. AB24	14	D4
High St.		
Granville Pl. AB10	23	G5
Gray Ct. AB15	22	C2
Gray St. AB10	23	G5
Gray St. Ms. AB10	23	G5
Great Northern Rd. AB24	13	G2
Great Southern Rd. AB10	24	A5
Great Southern Rd. AB11	24	A5
Great Southern Rd. AB12	30	A1
Great Western Pl. AB10	23	H4
Great Western Rd. AB10	23	F5
Green, The AB11	24	C2
Rennies Wynd		
Green, The (Port.) AB12	38	D4
Greenbank Cres. AB12	30	D1
Greenbank Pl. AB12	30	D1
Greenbank Rd. AB12	30	D1
Greenbrae Av. (Br.Don) AB23	11	E4
Greenbrae Circle (Br.Don) AB23	11	E3
Greenbrae Cres. (Br.Don) AB23	11	E3
Greenbrae Dr. (Br.Don) AB23	11	E3
Greenbrae Gdns. N. AB23	11	E3
Greenbrae Gdns. S. AB23	11	E3
Greenbrae Wk. (Br.Don) AB23	11	E3
Greenburn Dr. (Bucks.) AB21	8	B6
Greenburn Pk. (Bucks.) AB21	8	B6
Greenburn Rd. (Bucks.) AB21	8	C6
Greenburn Rd. N. AB21	8	A5
Greenburn Ter. (Bucks.) AB21	12	B1
Greenfern Av. AB16	12	D6
Greenfern Pl. AB16	12	D6
Greenfern Rd.		
Greenfern Rd. AB16	12	D6
Greenhole Pl. AB23	10	D5
Greenmore Gdns. AB24	14	B4
Greenwell Pl. AB12	25	E6
Greenwell Rd. AB12	25	E6
Gregness Gdns. AB11	25	E6
Greig Ct. AB25	5	C1
Greyhope Rd. AB11	25	G3
Greystone Pl. (Newt.), Stone. AB39	41	E4
Groats Rd. AB15	22	A3
Grosvenor Pl. AB25	4	A2
Grosvenor Ter. AB25	24	A2
Grosvenor Pl.		
Grove Cres. AB16	14	A6
Guestrow AB10	24	C2
Broad St.		
Guild St. AB11	5	D3
Gullymoss Gdns., Westh. AB32	17	E3
Gullymoss Pl., Westh. AB32	17	E3
Gullymoss Vw., Westh. AB32	17	E3

H

Hadden St. AB11	24	C2
Market St.		
Hallfield Cres. AB16	22	B1
Hallfield Rd. AB16	22	B1
Hamilton La. AB15	23	F2
Hamilton Pl.		
Hamilton Pl. AB15	23	F2
Hammerfield Av. AB10	23	F5
Hammersmith Rd. AB10	23	G5
Hanover St. AB11	5	E1
Harcourt Rd. AB15	23	F1
Hardgate AB10	24	A5
Hardgate AB11	24	A4
Hardgate La. AB10	24	A5
Hardgate		
Harehill Rd. (Br.Don) AB22	10	C6
Hareness Circle AB12	31	E3
Hareness Pk. AB12	31	E3
Hareness Rd. AB12	30	D3
Harlaw Pl. AB15	23	F4
Harlaw Rd. AB15	23	F4
Harlaw Ter. AB15	23	F4
Harley Ter. (Port.) AB12	39	G4
Harriet St. AB25	5	C2
Harris Dr. AB24	14	C3
Harrow Rd. AB24	15	E3
Harthill Pl. AB16	12	C6
Hartington Rd. AB10	23	G3
Harvest Hill, Westh. AB32	16	B4
Hasman Ter. (Co.Bay) AB12	37	G1
Spark Ter.		
Hawthorn Cres. AB16	13	F5
Hawthorn Ter. AB24	15	F6
Urquhart Pl.		
Hayfield Cres. AB24	14	A5
Hayfield Pl. AB24	14	A4
Hays Way, Westh. AB32	16	D4
Hayton Rd. AB24	14	B3
Hazel Dr., Westh. AB32	16	D5
Hazledene Rd. AB15	22	C4
Hazlehead Av. AB15	22	B3
Hazlehead Caravan Pk. AB15	22	A3
Hazlehead Cres. AB15	22	B3
Hazlehead Gdns. AB15	22	A3
Hazlehead Pl. AB15	22	B3
Hazlehead Rd. AB15	22	B3
Hazlehead Ter. AB15	22	A3
Headland Ct. AB10	29	H1
Headland Ter. (Newt.), Stone. AB39	41	E4
Villagelands Rd.		
Heather Pl. (Port.) AB12	38	D3
Heathfield Pk. (Newt.), Stone. AB39	40	D4
Heathryfold Circle AB16	13	E3
Heathryfold Dr. AB16	13	E3
Heathryfold Pl. AB16	13	E3
Henderson Dr., Westh. AB32	16	D5
Hermitage Av. AB12	14	D4
Hetherwick Rd. AB12	29	H3
High St. AB24	14	D4
Highgate Gdns. AB11	24	B5
Hill of Rubislaw AB15	22	D4
Hill St. AB25	4	B1
Hill Vw. Gdns. AB12	24	D6
Hill Vw. Pl. AB12	30	D1
Hillcrest Pl. AB16	13	G4
Cummings Pk. Circle		
Hillhead Rd. (Bield.) AB15	26	D3
Hillhead Rd. (Newt.), Stone. AB39	41	E4
Hillhead Ter. AB24	14	D5
Spital		
Hillocks Way (Bucks.) AB21	12	C2
Hillside Cres., Peter. AB14	32	D2
Hillside Cres., Westh. AB32	17	E3
Hillside Gdns., Westh. AB32	17	E3
Hillside Pl., Peter. AB14	32	D2
Hillside Rd., Peter. AB14	32	D3
Hillside Rd., Westh. AB32	17	E3
Hillside Ter. (Port.) AB12	39	E3
Hillside Vw., Westh. AB32	17	E3
Hillswick Rd. AB16	12	B6
Hillswick Wk. AB16	12	B6
Hilltop Av. (Cults) AB15	27	H2
Hilltop Av., Westh. AB32	16	D3
Hilltop Cres., Westh. AB32	16	D3
Hilltop Dr., Westh. AB32	16	D3
Hilltop Rd., Westh. AB32	17	E3
Hilltop Rd. (Cults) AB15	27	H2
Hillview Av., Westh. AB32	17	E3
Hillview Dr. (Cults) AB15	27	H3
Hillview Dr. (Cults) AB15	27	H2
Hillview Rd. AB12	24	D6
Hillview Rd. (Cults) AB15	27	H3
Hillview Rd., Peter. AB14	32	D3
Hillview Rd., Westh. AB32	17	E3
Hillview Ter. (Cults) AB15	27	H3
Hillylands Rd. AB16	22	C1
Hilton Av. AB24	13	H4
Hilton Circle AB24	14	A5
Hilton Ct. AB24	13	H4
Hilton Dr. AB24	14	A4
Hilton Pl. AB24	14	B4
Hilton Rd. AB24	13	H4
Hilton St. AB24	14	A5
Hilton Ter. AB24	14	A4
Hilton Wk. AB24	14	A4
Holburn Pl. AB10	23	H5
Holburn Rd. AB10	23	H4
Holburn St. AB10	24	A5
Holland Pl. AB25	14	C6
Holland St. AB25	14	C6
Hollybank Pl. AB11	24	A4
Holmhead Pl. (Bucks.) AB21	12	B2
Newhills Av.		
Homelea, Westh. AB32	16	B5
Hopecroft Av. (Bucks.) AB21	8	B6
Hopecroft Dr. (Bucks.) AB21	8	B6
Hopecroft Gdns. (Bucks.) AB21	12	B1

Name	Page	Grid
Hopecroft Ter. (Bucks.) AB21	8	B6
Hopetoun Av. (Bucks.) AB21	12	A1
Hopetoun Ct. (Bucks.) AB21	12	B1
Hopetoun Cres. (Bucks.) AB21	12	A1
Hopetoun Dr. (Bucks.) AB21	12	A1
Hopetoun Gra. (Bucks.) AB21	12	A1
Hopetoun Grn. (Bucks.) AB21	12	B1
Hopetoun Rd. (Bucks.) AB21	12	A1
Hopetoun Ter. (Bucks.) AB21	12	A1
Hosefield Av. AB15	23	G1
Hosefield Rd. AB15	23	G1
Howburn Pl. AB11	24	A4
Howe Moss Av. AB21	6	B3
Howe Moss Cres. AB21	6	B3
Howe Moss Dr. AB21	6	B4
Howe Moss Pl. AB21	6	B3
Howe Moss Rd. AB21	6	B3
Howe Moss Ter. AB21	6	C2
Howes Cres. AB16	12	D3
Howes Dr. AB16	12	D3
Howes Pk. AB16	13	E3
Howes Cres.		
Howes Pl. AB16	12	D3
Howes Cres.		
Howes Rd. (Bucks.) AB21	12	C3
Howes Vw. (Bucks.) AB21	12	C2
Howie La., Peter. AB14	33	E4
Hunter Pl. AB24	15	E6
Huntly St. AB10	4	B2
Hutcheon Ct. AB25	14	D6
Hutcheon Gdns. (Br.Don) AB23	15	E1
Hutcheon Low Dr. AB21	13	F2
Hutcheon Low Pl. AB21	13	G2
Hutcheon St. AB25	4	B1
Hutchison Ter. AB10	23	F6
Hutton La. AB16	13	E4
Byron Cres.		
Hutton Pl. AB16	13	E4
Huxterstone Ct. (Kings.) AB15	18	D5
Huxterstone Dr. (Kings.) AB15	18	D5
Huxterstone Pl. (Kings.) AB15	18	C5
Huxterstone Ter. (Kings.) AB15	18	D5
I		
Imperial Pl. AB11	24	C2
Guild St.		
Inchbrae Dr. AB10	29	E2
Inchbrae Rd. AB10	29	F2
Inchbrae Ter. AB10	29	E2
Inchgarth Rd. (Cults) AB15	28	C2
Ingram Wk. AB12	30	C3
Intown Rd. (Br.Don) AB23	11	F6
Invercauld Gdns. AB16	13	F5
Invercauld Pl. AB16	13	E5
Invercauld Rd.		
Invercauld Rd. AB16	13	E5
Inverdon Ct. AB24	15	E2
Inverurie Rd. (Bucks.) AB21	12	C1
Irvine Pl. AB10	23	H5
Isla Pl. AB16	12	D6
Ivanhoe Pl. AB10	29	E1
Ivanhoe Rd. AB10	29	E1
Ivanhoe Wk. AB10	29	E1
J		
Jacks Brae AB25	4	B2
Jackson Ter. AB24	15	E6
Urquhart La.		
Jamaica St. AB25	14	C6
James St. AB11	5	E2
Jamiesons Quay AB11	5	D3
Jasmine Pl. AB24	5	D1
Jasmine Ter. AB24	5	D1
Jasmine Way AB24	5	D1
Jesmond Av. (Br.Don) AB22	10	C4
Jesmond Av. N. (Br.Don) AB22	10	A4
Jesmond Circle (Br.Don) AB22	10	A3
Jesmond Dr. (Br.Don) AB22	10	C4
Jesmond Gdns. (Br.Don) AB22	10	A3
Jesmond Gro. (Br.Don) AB22	10	A3
Jesmond Rd. (Br.Don) AB22	10	B5
Jesmond Sq. (Br.Don) AB22	10	B5
Jesmond Sq. E. (Br.Don) AB22	10	B5
Jesmond Sq.		
Jesmond Sq. N. (Br.Don) AB22	10	B5
Jesmond Sq.		
Jesmond Sq. S. (Br.Don) AB22	10	B5
Jesmond Sq.		
John Arthur Ct. (Kings.) AB15	19	E6
John St. (Dyce) AB21	7	F4
John St. AB25	4	C1
Johns Pk. Pl. AB22	14	A1
Johnston Gdns. E., Peter. AB14	32	C2
Johnston Gdns. N., Peter. AB14	32	D2
Johnston Gdns. W., Peter. AB14	32	D2
Jopps La. AB25	5	C1
Juniper Pl. (Port.) AB12	38	C4
Jura Pl. AB16	22	A1
Justice Mill Brae AB11	24	A3
Justice Mill La.		
Justice Mill La. AB11	4	B3
Justice Port AB24	24	D1
Beach Boul.		
Justice St. AB11	5	D2
Jute St. AB24	14	D6
K		
Kaimhill Circle AB10	29	G1
Kaimhill Gdns. AB10	29	G1
Kaimhill Rd. AB10	29	F1
Keir Circle, Westh. AB32	16	C4
Kemnay Pl. AB15	22	C4
Kemp St. AB16	13	G3
Kenfield Cres. AB15	23	E5
Kenfield Pl. AB15	23	E5
Kennerty Ct., Peter. AB14	32	D4
Kennerty Mills Rd.		
Kennerty Mills Rd., Peter. AB14	32	D4
Kennerty Pk., Peter. AB14	32	D4
Kennerty Rd., Peter. AB14	32	C4
Kepplehills Dr. (Bucks.) AB21	12	B1
Kepplehills Rd. (Bucks.) AB21	12	B2
Kepplestone Av. AB15	23	E4
Kerloch Gdns. AB11	24	C5
Kerloch Pl. AB11	24	C6
Kettlehills Cres. AB16	13	F4
Kettlehills La. AB16	13	F4
Kettlehills Rd. AB16	13	E4
Kettock Gdns. (Br.Don) AB22	10	B5
Mundurno Rd.		
Kettocks Mill Rd. AB22	14	C2
Kidd St. AB10	4	B2
Kildrummy Rd. AB15	22	C4
Kilsyth Rd. AB12	30	C2
Kinaldie Cres. AB15	22	C4
Kincorth Circle AB12	30	A2
Kincorth Cres. AB12	30	B1
Kincorth Gdns. AB12	30	B1
Kincorth Land AB12	30	B2
Kincorth Pl. AB12	30	A1
King George VI Br. AB10	24	B6
King St. AB24	15	E5
King St. (Woodside) AB24	14	A3
King's Ct. AB24	14	B2
Auchinleck Rd.		
Kings Cres. AB24	15	E6
King's Cross AB15	23	E2
King's Cross Av. AB15	22	D3
King's Cross Rd. AB15	22	D3
King's Cross Ter. AB15	22	D3
King's Gate AB15	23	F2
Kings Rd. AB24	14	B2
Auchinleck Rd.		
Kingsford Rd. AB16	12	D6
Kingshill Av. AB15	23	E1
Kingshill Rd. AB15	23	E2
Kingshill Ter. AB15	23	E2
Kingsland Pl. AB25	4	C1
Kingswalk (Bucks.) AB21	12	C1
Kingsway (Bucks.) AB21	12	C2
Kingswells Av. (Kings.) AB15	18	D4
Kingswells Cres. (Kings.) AB15	18	D3
Kingswells Dr. (Kings.) AB15	18	C3
Kingswells Vw. (Kings.) AB15	18	D3
Kingswood Av. (Kings.) AB15	18	D4
Kingswood Cres. (Kings.) AB15	18	D4
Kingswood Dr. (Kings.) AB15	18	D4
Kingswood Gdns. (Kings.) AB15	18	D5
Kingswood Gro. (Kings.) AB15	18	C4
Kingswood Ms. (Kings.) AB15	18	C4
Kingswood Path (Kings.) AB15	18	D4
Kingswood Rd. (Kings.) AB15	18	D4
Kingswood Wk. (Kings.) AB15	18	D4
Kinkell Rd. AB15	22	C4
Kinmundy Av., Westh. AB32	17	E4
Kinmundy Dr., Westh. AB32	17	E4
Kinmundy Gdns., Westh. AB32	17	E4
Kinmundy Grn., Westh. AB32	17	F4
Kinnaird Pl. AB24	14	C3
Kinord Circle (Br.Don) AB22	14	D1
Kintore Gdns. AB25	24	A1
Kintore Pl.		
Kintore Pl. AB25	4	B1
Kirk Brae (Cults) AB15	28	A2
Kirk Brae Ct. (Cults) AB15	28	A2
Kirk Cres. N. (Cults) AB15	27	H2
Kirk Cres. S. (Cults) AB15	27	H2
Kirk Dr. (Cults) AB15	28	A2
Kirk Pl. (Cults) AB15	27	H2
Kirk Ter. (Cults) AB15	27	H2
Kirkbrae Av. (Cults) AB15	27	H2
Kirkbrae Dr. (Cults) AB15	27	G2
Kirkbrae Ms. (Cults) AB15	28	A2
Kirkbrae Vw. (Cults) AB15	27	H2
Kirkhill Dr. (Dyce) AB21	6	C2
Kirkhill Ind. Est. (Dyce) AB21	6	B3
Kirkhill Pl. AB11	25	E6
Kirkhill Pl. (Dyce) AB21	6	C4
Kirkhill Rd. AB11	24	D6
Kirkhill Rd. (Dyce) AB21	6	C3
Kirkside Ct., Westh. AB32	17	E4
Kirkton Av. AB21	7	E1
Kirkton Av., Westh. AB32	16	B4
Kirkton Dr. (Dyce) AB21	7	E2
Kirkton Gdns., Westh. AB32	16	B5
Kirkton Rd., Westh. AB32	16	B4
Kirkwall Av. AB16	12	B6
Kittybrewster Sq. AB25	14	B5
Kvaerner Village (Dyce) AB21	6	B2
L		
Laburnum Wk. AB16	13	H5
Lade Cres. (Bucks.) AB21	8	C5
Ladywell Pl. AB11	25	E5
Laird Gdns. (Dane.) AB22	10	A6
Lamond Pl. AB25	14	C6
Lang Stracht AB15	22	C1
Lang Stracht AB16	22	C1
Langdykes Cres. (Co.Bay) AB12	30	D5
Langdykes Dr. (Co.Bay) AB12	30	D5
Langdykes Rd. (Co.Bay) AB12	30	D5
Langdykes Way (Co.Bay) AB12	31	E5
Langstane Pl. AB11	4	C3
Larch Rd. AB12	13	G5
Larg Dr., Westh. AB32	16	B4
Laurel Av. (Br.Don) AB22	14	A1
Laurel Braes (Br.Don) AB22	14	A1
Laurel Dr. (Br.Don) AB22	13	H1
Laurel Gdns. (Br.Don) AB22	14	A1
Laurel Gro. (Br.Don) AB22	14	A1
Laurel La. (Br.Don) AB22	14	A1
Laurel Dr.		
Laurel Pk. (Br.Don) AB22	14	A1
Laurel Braes		
Laurel Pl. (Br.Don) AB22	13	H1
Laurel Rd. (Br.Don) AB22	13	H1
Laurel Ter. (Br.Don) AB22	14	A1
Laurel Vw. (Br.Don) AB22	13	H1
Laurel Wynd (Br.Don) AB22	14	A1
Laurelwood Av. AB25	14	B5
Laverock Way (Br.Don) AB22	10	D6
Glashieburn Way		
Laws Dr. AB12	30	A3
Laws Rd. AB12	30	A3
Lawsondale Av., Westh. AB32	17	F5
Lawsondale Dr., Westh. AB32	17	F5
Lawsondale Ter., Westh. AB32	17	F5
Lea Rig, Westh. AB32	16	B4
Leadside Rd. AB25	4	B2
Learney Pl. AB15	23	F4
Leddach Gdns., Westh. AB32	16	C4
Leddach Pl., Westh. AB32	16	C4
Leddach Rd., Westh. AB32	16	C4
Lee Cres. (Br.Don) AB22	10	A4
Lee Cres. N. (Br.Don) AB22	10	A3
Leggart Av. AB12	29	H2
Leggart Cres. AB12	29	H3
Leggart Pl. AB12	29	H2
Leggart Rd. AB12	29	H2
Leggart Ter. AB12	29	H2
Lemon Pl. AB24	24	D1
Park St.		
Lemon St. AB24	5	E1
Lerwick Rd. AB16	12	C6

Leslie Cres., Westh. AB32	16	C4
Leslie Rd. AB24	14	B4
Leslie Ter. AB25	14	C5
Lethen Wk. (Port.) AB12	38	C5
Lewis Ct. AB16	12	B6
Lewis Dr. AB16	12	B6
Lewis Rd. AB16	22	A1
Lewisvale, Peter. AB14	33	F3
Licklyhead Way (Dyce) AB21	7	G2
Netherview Av.		
Liddell Pl. AB21	7	F2
Lilac Pl. AB16	13	F5
Lilybank Rd. AB24	14	B4
Lime St. AB11	5	E2
Lindsay St. AB10	24	B2
Golden Sq.		
Links Pl. AB11	25	E2
Links Rd. AB11	25	E1
Links Rd. (Br.Don) AB23	15	F1
Links Rd. AB24	5	E1
Links St. AB11	25	E2
Links Vw. AB24	15	F5
Linksfield Ct. AB24	15	F4
Linksfield Gdns. AB24	15	E5
Linksfield Pl. AB24	15	E5
Linksfield Rd. AB24	15	E5
Lintmill Pl. AB16	12	D4
Lintmill Ter. AB16	12	D4
Lismore Gdns. AB16	12	B6
Taransay Rd.		
Little Belmont St. AB10	24	B2
Belmont St.		
Little Chapel St. AB10	24	A2
Chapel St.		
Littlejohn St. AB10	5	D1
Livingstone Ct. AB24	15	E3
Loanhead Pl. AB25	4	A1
Loanhead Ter. AB25	4	A1
Loanhead Wk. AB25	4	A1
Loch St. AB25	5	C1
Loch Vw., Westh. AB32	16	C3
Lochnagar Cres., Peter. AB14	33	E2
Lochnagar Rd. AB25	25	F5
Lochnagar Rd., Peter. AB14	33	E2
Lochside Av. (Br.Don) AB23	10	D4
Lochside Cres. (Br.Don) AB23	10	D4
Lochside Dr. (Br.Don) AB23	10	D4
Lochside Pl. (Br.Don) AB23	10	D4
Lochside Rd.		
Lochside Rd. (Br.Don) AB23	10	D5
Lochside Ter. (Br.Don) AB23	11	E4
Lochside Way (Br.Don) AB23	10	D4
Lochview Dr. (Br.Don) AB23	10	D4
Lochview Pl. (Br.Don) AB23	10	D4
Lochview Way (Br.Don) AB23	10	D4
Lodge Wk. AB11	24	C2
Union St.		
Logie Av. AB16	13	G2
Logie Gdns. AB16	13	G2
Logie Av.		
Logie Pl. AB16	13	F3
Logie Ter. AB16	13	F3
Loirsbank Rd. (Cults) AB15	28	A3
Loirston Av. (Co.Bay) AB12	30	D6
Loirston Cl. (Co. Bay) AB12	30	D6
Loirston Ct. (Co.Bay) AB12	30	D6
Loirston Cres. (Co.Bay) AB12	31	E6
Loirston Manor (Co.Bay) AB12	31	E6
Loirston Pl AB11	25	E5
Loirston Pl. (Co.Bay) AB12	31	E6
Loirston Rd. AB12	31	E6
Loirston Wk. (Co.Bay) AB12	30	D5
Loirston Way (Co.Bay) AB12	30	D5
Long Wk. Pl. AB16	13	F5
Long Wk. Rd. AB16	13	F5
Long Wk. Ter. AB16	13	F5
Longcairn Gdns. (Bucks.) AB21	12	B2
Middle Brae		
Longlands Pl. AB16	13	F5
Longview Ter. AB16	12	D3
Lord Hay's Ct. AB24	15	F2
Lord Hay's Gro. (Old Aberdeen) AB24	15	E2
Lossie Pl. AB16	12	D6
Louden Pl. (Dyce) AB21	7	G2
Louisville Av. AB15	23	F4
M		
Maberly St. AB25	4	C1

Macaulay Dr. (Craigiebuckler) AB15	22	C5
Macaulay Gdns. AB15	22	D5
Macaulay Pk. AB15	22	D5
Macaulay Pl. AB15	22	D5
Macaulay Wk. AB15	22	D5
Mackay Rd. AB12	30	A2
Mackenzie Pl. AB24	14	D4
High St.		
Mackie Pl. AB10	4	B2
Magdala Pl. AB25	24	A1
Short Loanings		
Maidencraig Pl. AB16	22	B1
Mains Circle, Westh. AB32	17	F4
Mains Ct., Westh. AB32	17	F4
Mains Dr., Westh. AB32	17	F4
Mains Gdns., Westh. AB32	17	F4
Mains Vw., Westh. AB32	17	F3
Maitlands Quay AB11	25	E4
Sinclair Rd.		
Malcolm Rd. (Bucks.) AB21	12	D1
Manor Av. AB16	13	F3
Manor Dr. AB16	13	F3
Manor Pk. Caravan Pk. AB16	13	F2
Manor Pl. (Cults) AB15	28	A3
Manor Ter. AB16	13	G3
Manor Wk. AB16	13	F3
Manse Rd. (Cults) AB15	27	G3
Mansefield Pl. AB11	24	D5
Mansefield Rd. AB11	25	E4
Maple Pl. (Co.Bay) AB12	37	F1
Marchbank Rd. (Bield.) AB15	27	F4
Marchburn Av. AB16	13	E4
Marchburn Ct. AB16	12	D3
Marchburn Ct. Rd.		
Marchburn Ct. Rd. AB16	12	D3
Marchburn Cres. AB16	13	E3
Marchburn Dr. AB16	13	E3
Marchburn Pl. AB16	13	E3
Marchburn Rd. AB16	13	E3
Marchburn Ter. AB16	13	F3
Marchburn Dr.		
Marchmont Pl. AB12	31	E5
Marchmont St. AB12	31	E5
Margaret Pl. AB10	23	H6
Margaret St. AB10	24	A2
Rose St.		
Marine Ct. AB11	24	B4
Marine Ter.		
Marine La. AB11	24	B4
Abbotsford La.		
Marine Pl. AB11	24	B4
South Crown St.		
Marine Ter. AB11	24	B4
Marine Ter. (Muchalls), Stone. AB39	40	C6
Marischal Ct. AB11	24	C2
Justice St.		
Marischal Gdns. (Bucks.) AB21	12	B2
Marischal St. AB11	5	D2
Mark Bush Ct. AB12	30	A1
Market La. AB24	14	D4
High St.		
Market St. AB11	5	D2
Market St. (Bucks.) AB21	7	F6
Marlpool Pl. (Bucks.) AB21	12	B2
Marischal Gdns.		
Marquis Rd. AB24	14	B3
Marsh Pl. (Port.) AB12	38	D4
Martins La. AB11	24	C2
Rennies Wynd		
Maryculter Br. (Maryculter) AB12	33	H4
Maryville Pk. AB15	22	D2
Anderson Dr.		
Maryville Pl. AB15	22	D2
Marywell Pk. Homes (Nigg) AB12	36	B5
Marywell St. AB11	5	C3
Mastrick Cl. AB16	13	F6
Mastrick Dr. AB16	13	E6
Mastrick Junct. AB16	13	E6
Mastrick Land AB16	13	E6
Mastrick Rd.		
Mastrick Rd. AB16	13	E6
Matthew Pl. (Bucks.) AB21	12	C1
Matthews Quay AB11	25	E3
Matthews Rd. AB12	30	A3
May Baird Av. AB25	14	B5
Ashgrove Rd.		
Mayfield Gdns. AB15	23	F4

McCombies Ct. AB10	24	A3
Union St.		
Meadow Ct. AB24	14	B2
Gordon's Mills Cres.		
Meadow La. AB24	14	C2
Meadow Pl. AB24	14	B2
Meadowlands Av., Westh. AB32	17	E2
Meadowlands Dr.		
Meadowlands Cl., Westh. AB32	17	E2
Meadowlands Ct., Westh. AB32	17	E2
Meadowlands Cres., Westh. AB32	17	E2
Meadowlands Dr., Westh. AB32	16	D2
Meadowlands Pk., Westh. AB32	16	D2
Meadowlands Pl., Westh. AB32	16	D2
Meadowlands Way, Westh. AB32	17	E2
Meadows, The, Mill. AB13	26	B4
Mealmarket St. AB24	5	D1
Mearns Quay AB11	25	E3
Mearns St. AB11	5	E2
Meikle Gdns., Westh. AB32	16	D4
Melrose Wk., Peter. AB14	32	D3
Menzies Rd. AB11	24	D4
Merkland La. AB24	15	F5
Merkland Pl. AB24	15	E5
Merkland Rd. AB24	15	E5
Merkland Rd. E. AB24	15	E5
Meston Wk. AB24	14	D4
Mid Stocket Rd. AB15	23	E1
Midchingle Rd. AB11	5	E3
Middle Brae (Bucks.) AB21	12	A2
Middle Row AB11	25	F3
Middlefield Cres. AB24	13	H3
Middlefield Pl. AB16	13	G3
Middlefield Pl. AB24	13	G3
Middlefield Ter. AB24	13	H3
Middlefield Wk. AB24	13	H4
Hilton Rd.		
Middlemuir Pl. (Bucks.) AB21	12	B2
Middleton Circle (Br.Don) AB22	10	A4
Middleton Cl. (Br.Don) AB22	10	A4
Middleton Cres. (Br.Don) AB22	10	A4
Middleton Dr. (Br.Don) AB22	10	A4
Middleton Gro. (Br.Don) AB22	10	A4
Middleton Path (Br.Don) AB22	10	A4
Middleton Pl. (Br.Don) AB22	10	D6
Glashieburn Way		
Middleton Rd. (Br.Don) AB22	10	A4
Middleton Ter. (Br.Don) AB22	10	A4
Middleton Way (Br.Don) AB22	10	A4
Midmar Cres. (Kings.) AB15	18	D3
Midmar Pk. (Kings.) AB15	18	D3
Midmar Vw. (Kings.) AB15	18	D4
Midmar Wk. (Kings.) AB15	18	D3
Midstocket Ms. AB15	23	E1
Mid Stocket Rd.		
Migvie Av. (Kings.) AB15	18	D3
Migvie Gdns. (Kings.) AB15	18	D3
Migvie Gro. (Kings.) AB15	18	D3
Migvie Lea (Kings.) AB15	18	D3
Mile-End Av. AB15	23	G1
Mile-End La. AB15	23	G1
Mile-End Pl. AB15	23	G1
Mill Ct. (Woodside) AB24	13	H2
Mill Lade Wynd (Br.Don) AB22	13	G1
Millarsmires End (Br.Don) AB22	10	C5
Mundurno Rd.		
Millarsmires Way AB22	10	C5
Mundurno Rd.		
Millbank La. AB25	14	C6
Millbank Pl. AB25	14	C6
Millburn St. AB11	24	B4
Millden Rd. (Cults) AB15	28	A2
Milleath Wk. (Dyce) AB21	7	G2
Balloch Way		
Miller St. AB11	5	E2
Millgrove Rd. (Bucks.) AB21	8	C5
Stoneywood Rd.		
Millhill Brae (Bucks.) AB21	8	C6
Millside Dr., Peter. AB14	32	D3
Millside Rd., Peter. AB14	32	C3
Millside St. AB14	32	C3
Millside Ter., Peter. AB14	32	C3
Milltimber Brae, Mill. AB13	26	A6
Milltimber Brae E., Mill. AB13	26	A6
Milton Br. (Maryculter) AB12	33	H4
Miltonfold (Bucks.) AB21	12	C1
Miltonfold Ct. (Bucks.) AB21	12	C1
Miltonfold		

Minden Cl. (Br.Don) AB23	11	F6
Minister La. AB10	24	A2
Summer St.		
Minto Av. (Altens Ind. Est.) AB12	31	F2
Minto Dr. (Altens Ind. Est.) AB12	31	F3
Minto Rd. (Altens Ind. Est.) AB12	31	F3
Moir Av. AB16	13	G4
Moir Cres. AB16	13	G4
Moir Dr. AB16	13	G5
Moir Grn. AB16	13	G4
Monach Ter. AB16	21	H1
Monduff Rd. (Muchalls), Stone. AB39	40	C6
Monearn Gdns., Mill. AB13	26	B5
Montgomery Cres. AB24	14	B2
Montgomery Rd. AB24	14	B2
Montrose Cl. (Dyce) AB21	6	C4
Montrose Dr. AB10	29	F2
Montrose Rd. (Dyce) AB21	6	C4
Montrose Way (Dyce) AB21	6	C4
Monymusk Ter. AB15	22	B4
Moor Pl. (Port.) AB12	39	E3
Moray Pl. AB15	23	E2
Morgan Rd. AB16	13	H5
Morningfield Rd. AB15	23	E2
Morningside Av. AB10	29	F1
Morningside Cres. AB10	29	F1
Morningside Gdns. AB10	23	F6
Morningside Gro. AB10	23	F6
Morningside Rd.		
Morningside La. AB10	23	F6
Morningside Pl. AB10	23	F6
Morningside Rd. AB10	23	F6
Morningside Ter. AB10	23	F6
Morrison Dr. AB10	29	E1
Morrisons Br. (Cults) AB15	28	B3
Mortimer Dr. AB15	22	A3
Mortimer Pl. AB15	22	B3
Morven Circle, Westh. AB32	16	D4
Morven Ct. AB11	25	F5
Balnagask Circle		
Morven Cres., Westh. AB32	16	D4
Morven Dr., Westh. AB32	16	D4
Morven Gdns., Westh. AB32	16	D4
Morven Pl. AB11	24	D5
Mosman Gdns. AB24	13	H4
Mosman Pl. AB24	13	H4
Mosscroft Av., Westh. AB32	16	C6
Mosside Ct., Westh. AB32	16	D5
Brimmond Dr.		
Mosside Cres. (Port.) AB12	38	D3
Mosside Pl. (Port.) AB12	38	D3
Mosside Pl., Westh. AB32	16	D5
Brimmond Dr.		
Mosside Way (Bucks.) AB21	12	B2
Newhills Av.		
Mount Pleasant (Br.Don) AB23	15	E1
Mount St. AB25	4	B1
Mounthooly AB24	15	E6
Mounthooly Way AB24	15	E6
Mountview Gdns. AB25	24	A1
Mount St.		
Mugiemoss Ct. (Bucks.) AB21	12	D1
Mugiemoss Rd.		
Mugiemoss Rd. AB21	13	F2
Muirend Rd. (Port.) AB12	38	D3
Muirfield Pl. AB16	13	F6
Willowpark Pl.		
Muirfield Rd. AB16	13	F6
Mastrick Dr.		
Muirton Cres. (Dyce) AB21	7	G2
Mull Way AB16	22	A1
Mundurno Rd. (Br.Don) AB22	10	B6
Murcar Ind. Est. (Br.Don) AB23	11	F3
Murray Ct. AB24	13	H2
Murray Rd. (Newt.), Stone. AB39	41	E3
Murray Ter. AB11	24	B5
Murtle Den Rd., Mill. AB13	26	D4
Myrtle Ter. (Port.) AB12	38	C4

N

Nellfield Pl. AB10	23	H4
Nelson Ct. AB24	15	E6
Nelson La. AB24	15	E6
Nelson St. AB24	15	E6
Ness Pl. AB16	12	D6
Netherbrae (Bucks.) AB21	12	B2
Kepplehills Rd.		
Netherby Rd. (Cults) AB15	27	H3
Netherhills Av. (Bucks.) AB21	12	B2
Netherhills Pl. (Bucks.) AB21	12	B2
Netherkirkgate AB10	24	C2
Union St.		
Nethermains Rd. (Muchalls), Stone. AB39	40	C6
Netherview Av. (Dyce) AB21	7	G3
Netherview Pl. (Dyce) AB21	7	F3
Netherview Rd. (Dyce) AB21	7	F3
Nevis Business Pk. (Br.Don) AB22	10	B6
New Pk. Pl. AB16	13	E6
New Pk. Rd. AB16	13	E6
New Pier Rd. AB11	25	F3
Newburgh Circle (Br.Don) AB22	10	B4
Newburgh Cres. (Br.Don) AB22	10	C4
Newburgh Dr. (Br.Don) AB22	10	B4
Newburgh Path (Br.Don) AB22	10	B4
Newburgh Pl. (Br.Don) AB22	10	C4
Newburgh Rd. (Br.Don) AB22	10	C4
Newburgh St. (Br.Don) AB22	10	B4
Newburgh Way (Br.Don) AB22	10	B4
Newhills Av. AB21	12	B2
Newlands Av. AB10	23	G6
Newlands Cres. AB10	23	G6
Newton of Murcar Ind. Est. AB23	11	E2
Newton Pl. (Newt.), Stone. AB39	41	E3
Newton Rd.		
Newton Rd. AB16	13	G3
Newton Rd. (Dyce) AB21	6	C3
Newton Rd. (Newt.), Stone. AB39	41	E3
Newton Ter. (Bucks.) AB21	12	D1
Newtonhill Rd. (Newt.), Stone. AB39	40	D4
Nicol Pl. (Port.) AB12	39	E3
Nigg Holiday Pk. (Nigg) AB12	30	D2
Nigg Kirk Rd. AB12	30	D2
Nigg Way AB12	30	A4
Ninian Pl. (Port.) AB12	39	E2
Ninian Rd. (Dyce) AB21	6	C3
Norfolk Rd. AB10	23	G5
North Anderson Dr. AB15	13	G5
North Anderson Dr. AB16	13	G5
North Balnagask Rd. AB11	25	F4
North Deeside Rd. AB15	28	C2
North Deeside Rd., Mill. AB13	26	B6
North Deeside Rd., Peter. AB14	32	D3
North Donside Rd. (Br.Don) AB23	11	E6
North Esp. E. AB11	5	E3
North Esp. W. AB11	24	C4
North Grampian Circle AB11	24	D5
North St. Andrew St. AB25	24	B1
St. Andrew St.		
North Silver St. AB10	4	C2
North Sq. AB11	25	F3
North Stocket La. AB16	13	F5
Lilac Pl.		
Northburn Av. AB15	22	C3
Northburn La. AB15	22	C3
Northcote Av. AB15	22	D6
Northcote Cres. AB15	22	D6
Northcote Hill AB15	28	D1
Northcote Pk. AB15	28	D1
Northcote Rd. AB15	28	D1
Northfield Ind. Est. AB16	13	F4
Northfield Pl. AB25	4	B2
Northsea Ct. AB24	15	F3
Novar Pl. AB25	4	B1
Nursery La. AB16	13	G5
West Cairncry Rd.		

O

Oak Cres., Westh. AB32	16	D5
Oak Dr. (Port.) AB12	38	D5
Oakdale Ter. AB15	23	F6
St. John's Ter.		
Oakhill Cres. AB15	23	F2
Oakhill Rd. AB15	23	E2
Old Ch. Rd. AB11	24	D6
Old Coast Rd. (Port.) AB12	39	F5
Old Ferry Rd. (Bield.) AB15	27	F4
Old Ford Rd. AB11	24	C4
Old Inn Rd. (Port.) AB12	39	H2
Old Mill Rd. (Newt.), Stone. AB39	40	D4
Old Skene Rd. (Kings.) AB15	19	E6
Old Skene Rd., Westh. AB32	16	C4
Oldcroft Ct. AB16	13	G6
Castleton Dr.		
Oldcroft Pl. AB16	13	G6
Oldcroft Ter. AB16	13	G6
Oldfold Av., Mill. AB13	26	B4
Oldfold Cres., Mill. AB13	26	B4
Oldfold Dr., Mill. AB13	26	B4
Oldfold Pk., Mill. AB13	26	B4
Oldfold Pl., Mill. AB13	26	B4
Oldfold Wk., Mill. AB13	26	B4
Oldman Rd. AB12	33	H6
Oldmeldrum Rd. AB21	12	D1
Oldmill Rd. AB11	24	B4
Bon Accord St.		
Oldtown Pl. AB16	13	E3
Oldtown Ter. AB16	13	E3
Orchard, The AB24	14	D5
Spital Wk.		
Orchard La. AB24	15	E5
Orchard Pl.		
Orchard Pl. AB24	14	D5
Orchard Pl. AB24	15	E5
Orchard St. AB24	14	D5
Orchard Wk. AB24	14	D5
Ord St. AB15	22	D3
Oriel Ter., Peter. AB14	32	D3
Station Rd. W.		
Orkney Av. AB16	12	B6
Osborne Pl. AB25	23	G2
Oscar Pl. AB11	24	D5
Oscar Rd. AB11	24	D5
Overhill Gdns. (Br.Don) AB22	10	C6
Overhills Wk. (Bucks.) AB21	12	B2
Middle Brae		
Overton Av. (Dyce) AB21	7	G4
Overton Circle (Dyce) AB21	7	G4
Overton Cres. (Dyce) AB21	7	G4
Overton Pk. (Dyce) AB21	7	G4
Overton Wk. (Dyce) AB21	7	G4
Overton Way (Dyce) AB21	7	F4
Oyne Rd. AB15	22	C4

P

Paddock, The, Peter. AB14	32	D4
Palmerston Pl. AB11	24	C4
Palmerston Rd. AB11	24	C4
Park Brae (Cults) AB15	28	A3
Park La. AB24	24	D1
Princes St.		
Park Pl. AB24	24	C1
Park St.		
Park Pl. (Newt.), Stone. AB39	40	D4
Park Rd. (Cults) AB15	28	A3
Park Rd. AB24	15	F6
Park St. AB24	5	E1
Park Vw. (Br.Don) AB23	11	E6
Gordon Rd.		
Parkhead Gdns. (Bucks.) AB21	12	B2
Clashbog Pl.		
Parkhill Av. (Dyce) AB21	7	G4
Parkhill Circle (Dyce) AB21	7	F4
Parkhill Ct. (Dyce) AB21	7	G2
Balloch Way		
Parkhill Cres. (Dyce) AB21	7	G4
Parkhill Way (Dyce) AB21	7	F4
Parkside, Westh. AB32	16	D5
Parkway, The (Br.Don) AB22	9	G6
Parkway, The (Br.Don) AB23	10	B6
Parkway E. AB23	11	F5
Partan Skelly Av. (Co.Bay) AB12	30	D6
Partan Skelly Way (Co.Bay) AB12	30	D6
Patagonian Ct. AB10	24	B2
Belmont St.		
Peacocks Cl. AB24	24	C1
East N. St.		
Peat Way (Port.) AB12	38	D3
Pennan Rd. AB24	14	C2
Pentland Cres. AB11	25	F5
Pentland Pl. AB11	25	F5
Pentland Rd. AB11	25	F4
Persley Br. AB22	13	F1
Persley Cres. AB16	13	G3
Persley Pk. Caravan Pk. (Bucks.) AB21	13	F2
Perwinnes Path (Br.Don) AB22	10	D6
Glashieburn Way		
Pheppie Rd. (Muchalls), Stone. AB39	40	C6
Phoenix Pl. (Bucks.) AB21	7	G6
Picardy Ct. AB10	24	A3
Rose St.		
Picktillum Av. AB25	14	B5
Picktillum Pl. AB25	14	B5
Pilot Sq. AB11	25	F3

Pinecrest Circle (Bield.) AB15	27	F2
Pinecrest Dr. (Bield.) AB15	27	E2
Pinecrest Gdns. (Bield.) AB15	27	E2
Pinecrest Wk. (Bield.) AB15	27	E3
Pinewood Av. AB15	22	B5
Pinewood Pl. (Co.Bay) AB12	31	E6
Pinewood Pl. AB15	22	B5
Pinewood Rd. AB15	22	B5
Pinewood Ter. AB15	22	C5
Piper Pl. (Port.) AB12	39	E2
Pirie's Ct. AB24	14	B4
Pirie's La. AB24	14	B4
Pitdourie Wk. (Bucks.) AB21	12	B2
Newhills Av.		
Pitfichie La. (Dyce) AB21	7	G2
Tornashean Gdns.		
Pitfichie Pl. AB21	7	G2
Pitfodels Sta. Rd. (Cults) AB15	28	D2
Pitmedden Av. (Dyce) AB21	7	F2
Pitmedden Cres. AB10	29	G2
Pitmedden Dr. (Dyce) AB21	7	F2
Pitmedden Ind. Est. (Dyce) AB21	7	E2
Pitmedden Ms. (Dyce) AB21	7	F2
Pitmedden Rd. AB10	29	G1
Pitmedden Rd. AB21	7	E1
Pitmedden Ter. AB10	29	G1
Pitmedden Way (Dyce) AB21	7	F2
Pitstruan Pl. AB10	23	H4
Pitstruan Ter. AB10	23	H5
Pittengullies Brae, Peter. AB14	33	F3
Pittengullies Circle, Peter. AB14	33	F3
Pittodrie La. AB24	15	E5
Pittodrie Pl. AB24	15	E5
Pittodrie St. AB24	15	E5
Plane Tree Rd. AB16	13	G5
Plover Ct. (Newt.), Stone. AB39	41	E3
Pocra Quay AB11	25	F3
Polmuir Av. AB11	24	B5
Polmuir Pl. AB11	24	B5
Polmuir Rd. AB11	24	B4
Polo Gdns. (Bucks.) AB21	7	G6
Polston Rd. AB12	33	H6
Polwarth Rd. AB11	24	C5
Poplar Rd. AB16	13	G5
Larch Rd.		
Portal Cres. AB24	14	C3
Portal Ter. AB24	14	C4
Porthill Ct. AB25	24	C1
Gallowgate		
Portland St. AB11	5	C3
Portree Av. AB16	12	C6
Poultry Mkt. La. AB10	24	C2
Queen St.		
Powis Circle AB24	14	C4
Powis Cres. AB24	14	C4
Powis La. AB25	14	C6
Powis Pl. AB25	14	C6
Powis Ter. AB25	14	C5
Poynernook Rd. AB11	5	D3
Primrosebank Av. (Cults) AB15	28	B3
Primrosebank Dr. (Cults) AB15	28	B3
Primrosehill Av. AB15	28	B3
Primrosehill Dr. AB24	14	B4
Primrosehill Gdns. AB24	14	B4
Primrosehill Pl. AB24	14	B4
Primrosehill Rd. AB15	28	B3
Prince Arthur St. AB10	4	A2
Princes St. AB24	5	D1
Princess Cres. (Dyce) AB21	7	G3
Princess Dr. (Dyce) AB21	7	G2
Princess Pl. (Dyce) AB21	7	G2
Princess Rd. (Dyce) AB21	7	G2
Princess Ter. (Dyce) AB21	7	G2
Princess Cres.		
Princess Wk. (Dyce) AB21	7	G2
Princess Rd.		
Princess Way (Dyce) AB21	7	G2
Princess Cres.		
Printfield Ter. AB24	14	B3
Printfield Wk. AB24	14	A3
Priory Pk., Peter. AB14	33	E3
Privet Hedges AB16	13	G5
Promenade Ct. AB24	15	F4
Prospect Ct. AB11	24	C5
Prospect Ter. AB11	24	C4
Prospect Ter. (Bucks.) AB21	8	C5
Prospecthill Rd. (Bield.) AB15	27	F4
Provost Fraser Dr. AB16	13	F5

Provost Graham Av. AB15	22	B3
Provost Hogg Ct. AB11	25	F4
Provost Mitchell Circle (Br.Don) AB23	11	E2
Dubford Rd.		
Provost Rust Dr. AB16	13	F3
Provost Watt Dr. AB12	30	B1
Puffin Ct. (Newt.), Stone. AB39	41	E3

Q

Quarry Ct. (Cults) AB15	27	G3
Quarry Pl. AB16	13	E4
Quarry Rd. (Cults) AB15	27	G3
Quarry Rd. AB16	13	E4
Queen Elizabeth II Br. AB11	24	C4
Queen St. AB10	5	D2
Queen St. (Woodside) AB24	14	A3
Queens Av. AB15	23	E4
Queens Ct. AB15	23	E4
Queen's Cross AB15	23	G3
Queens Den AB15	22	A2
Queens Gdns. AB15	23	G3
Queen's Gate AB15	23	F3
Queens La. N. AB15	23	G3
Queens La. S. AB10	23	F3
Queens La. S. AB15	23	F3
Queens Links Leisure Pk. AB24	25	E1
Queen's Rd. AB15	22	D3
Queens Ter. AB10	4	A3

R

Raasay Gdns. AB16	22	A1
Raeburn Pl. AB25	4	B1
Raeden Av. AB15	23	F1
Raeden Ct. AB15	23	E1
Raeden Cres. AB15	23	E1
Raeden Pk. Rd. AB15	23	F1
Raeden Pl. AB15	23	E1
Raeholm Rd. (Br.Don) AB22	10	B6
Raik Rd. AB11	5	D3
Ramsay Cres. AB10	29	F1
Ramsay Gdns. AB10	29	F2
Ramsay Pl. AB10	29	F2
Rappahouse End (Br.Don) AB22	10	C6
Silverburn Rd.		
Rattray Pl. AB24	14	C2
Raxton Pl. (Dyce) AB21	7	G2
Redmoss Av. AB12	30	D3
Redmoss Pk. AB12	30	D3
Redmoss Pl. AB12	30	C3
Redmoss Rd. AB12	30	A6
Redmoss Ter. AB12	30	D3
Redmoss Wk. AB12	30	D3
Redwood Cres. (Co.Bay) AB12	37	G1
Regensburg Ct. AB16	12	D6
Regent Ct. AB24	15	F4
Regent Quay AB11	5	E2
Regent Rd. AB11	5	E3
Regent Wk. AB24	15	E4
Rennies Wynd AB11	5	D2
Richmond Ct. AB25	24	A1
Richmond Ter.		
Richmond St. AB25	4	B1
Richmond Ter. AB25	4	B1
Richmond Wk. AB25	4	B1
Richmondhill Ct. AB15	23	F1
Richmondhill Gdns. AB15	23	F1
Richmondhill Pl. AB15	23	F2
Richmondhill Rd. AB15	23	F2
Ridgeway Gro. (Dane.) AB22	10	A6
Valentine Dr.		
Ritchie Pl. AB24	14	B2
Ritchie Pl. (Muchalls), Stone. AB39	40	C6
Riverside Dr. AB10	24	A6
Riverside Dr. AB11	24	C6
Riverside Ter. AB10	23	H6
Riverview Dr. (Dyce) AB21	7	G2
Robertson Smith Ct. AB12	30	C3
Nigg Way		
Robertston Pl., Mill. AB13	26	B5
Rockall Pl. AB11	25	E5
Rockall Rd. AB11	25	E5
Rocklands Rd. (Cults) AB15	28	B2
Rodger's Wk. AB25	4	C1
Ronaldsay Rd. AB15	22	A1
Swannay Rd.		
Ronaldsay Sq. AB15	22	A1
Swannay Rd.		

Rose Ho. (Hazlehead) AB15	22	B3
Hazlehead Rd.		
Rose Pl. AB10	24	A2
Rose St.		
Rose St. AB10	4	B2
Rosebank Gdns. AB11	24	B3
Rosebank Ter.		
Rosebank Pl. AB11	24	A4
Rosebank Ter. AB11	24	B4
Rosebery St. AB15	23	F1
Rosehill Av. AB24	13	H4
Rosehill Ct. AB16	13	G5
Rosehill Cres. AB24	14	A4
Rosehill Dr. AB24	13	H4
Rosehill Pl. AB24	14	A4
Rosehill Ter. AB24	14	A4
Rosemount Pl. AB25	4	A1
Rosemount Sq. AB25	24	A1
Richmond St.		
Rosemount Ter. AB25	4	B1
Rosemount Viaduct AB25	4	B1
Rosewell Dr. AB15	22	D2
Rosewell Gdns. AB15	22	D2
Rosewell Ho. AB15	22	D2
Rosewell Pk. AB15	22	D2
Rosewell Pl. AB15	22	D2
Rosewell Ter. AB15	22	D2
Rosewood Av. AB12	30	C3
Roslin Pl. AB24	5	E1
Roslin St. AB24	15	F6
Roslin Ter. AB24	15	E6
Ross Cres. AB16	13	F6
Rousay Dr. AB15	22	B1
Rousay Pl. AB15	22	B1
Eday Rd.		
Rousay Ter. AB15	22	B1
Rousay Dr.		
Rowan Dr., Westh. AB32	16	C5
Rowan Rd. AB16	13	H5
Rowanbank Rd. (Port.) AB12	38	D3
Royfold Cres. AB15	23	E3
Rubislaw Den Gdns. AB15	23	E3
Rubislaw Den N. AB15	23	E3
Rubislaw Den S. AB15	23	E3
Rubislaw Pk. Cres. AB15	22	D4
Rubislaw Pk. Rd. AB15	22	D4
Rubislaw Pl. AB10	4	A3
Rubislaw Ter. AB10	4	A3
Rubislaw Ter. La. AB10	4	A3
Ruby La. AB10	24	B2
North Silver St.		
Ruby Pl. AB10	24	B2
North Silver St.		
Russell Rd. AB11	24	C4
Ruthrie Ct. AB10	23	G6
Ruthrie Gdns. AB10	29	G1
Ruthrie Rd. AB10	29	G1
Ruthrie Ter. AB10	29	G1
Ruthriehill Rd. (Bucks.) AB21	8	C5
Ruthrieston Circle AB10	23	H6
Ruthrieston Cres. AB10	23	H6
Ruthrieston Gdns. AB10	29	H1
Ruthrieston Pl. AB10	23	H6
Ruthrieston Rd. AB10	23	G6
Ruthrieston Ter. AB10	29	H1

S

St. Andrew Ct. AB25	24	B1
St. Andrew St.		
St. Andrew St. AB25	5	C1
St. Andrews Ter. (Newt.), Stone. AB39	40	D3
St. Anne's Cres. (Newt.), Stone. AB39	40	D2
St. Anne's Wynd (Newt.), Stone. AB39	40	D2
St. Catharines Wynd AB11	24	A3
Union St.		
St. Clair St. AB24	5	D1
St. Clement St. AB11	5	E2
St. Clements Pl. AB11	25	E2
St. Clement St.		
St. Crispin's Rd. (Newt.), Stone. AB39	40	D4
St. Devenicks Cres. (Cults) AB15	28	A3
St. Devenick's Pl. (Cults) AB15	28	A3
St. Devenick's Ter. (Cults) AB15	28	A3
St. Fitticks Rd. AB11	25	E4
St. Johns Pl. AB11	24	B3
Academy St.		
St. John's Rd. (Bucks.) AB21	12	C1

St. John's Ter. AB15 — 23 E6
St. John's Wk. (Newt.), Stone. AB39 — 40 D2
St. Machar Ct. AB24 — 14 B2
  Montgomery Cres.
St. Machar Dr. AB24 — 14 C4
St. Machar Ind. Est. AB24 — 14 C3
St. Machar Pl. AB24 — 15 E4
St. Machar Rd. AB24 — 14 C3
St. Margarets Pl. AB15 — 22 D2
St. Mary's Ct. AB10 — 24 B2
  Union Wynd
St. Mary's Pl. AB11 — 5 C3
St. Marys Pl., Peter. AB14 — 32 D3
  North Deeside Rd.
St. Michael's Cres. (Newt.), Stone. — 40 D3
  AB39
St. Michael's Pl. (Newt.), Stone. AB39 — 40 D3
St. Michael's Rd. (Newt.), Stone. — 40 D3
  AB39
St. Michael's Wk. (Newt.), Stone. — 40 D3
  AB39
St. Michael's Way (Newt.), Stone. — 40 D3
  AB39
St. Nathan's Rd. (Newt.), Stone. AB39 — 40 D3
St. Nicholas La. AB10 — 24 C2
  Schoolhill
St. Nicholas Shopping Cen. AB10 — 24 C2
  Schoolhill
St. Nicholas St. AB10 — 24 C2
  Schoolhill
St. Ninians Ct. AB24 — 15 E3
St. Ninians Pl. AB24 — 15 E2
St. Paul St. AB25 — 24 C1
  Gallowgate
St. Peter La. AB24 — 15 E6
St. Peter St. AB24 — 15 E6
St. Peter's Gate AB24 — 14 D5
St. Peter's Pl. AB24 — 15 E5
St. Peter's Rd. (Newt.), Stone. AB39 — 40 D3
St. Peters Ter., Peter. AB14 — 32 D3
St. Ronan's Circle, Peter. AB14 — 33 E2
St. Ronan's Cres., Peter. AB14 — 33 F2
St. Ronan's Dr., Peter. AB14 — 33 F3
St. Ronan's Pl., Peter. AB14 — 33 F3
St. Swithin Row AB10 — 23 G3
St. Swithin St. AB10 — 23 G3
St. Ternan's Rd. (Newt.), Stone. AB39 — 40 D4
Salisbury Ct. AB10 — 23 G5
Salisbury Pl. AB10 — 23 H5
Salisbury Ter. AB10 — 23 G5
Samphrey Rd. AB15 — 21 H2
Sanday Rd. AB15 — 22 C2
Sanderling Ct. (Newt.), Stone. AB39 — 41 E3
Sandilands Dr. AB24 — 14 B3
Scalpay Wk. AB16 — 21 H1
School Av. AB24 — 15 E4
School Cres., Peter. AB14 — 33 E3
School Dr. AB24 — 15 E4
School La., Peter. AB14 — 33 E3
School Pl. AB24 — 15 E4
  School Dr.
School Rd. (Cults) AB15 — 28 A3
School Rd. AB24 — 15 E4
School Rd., Peter. AB14 — 33 E3
School Ter. AB24 — 15 E4
School Wk. AB24 — 15 F4
Schoolhill AB10 — 5 C2
Schoolhill (Port.) AB12 — 38 D1
Sclattie Circle (Bucks.) AB21 — 12 B1
Sclattie Cres. (Bucks.) AB21 — 12 B1
Sclattie Pk. (Bucks.) AB21 — 12 B2
Sclattie Pl. (Bucks.) AB21 — 12 B2
Sclattie Wk. (Bucks.) AB21 — 12 B2
Scotstown Gdns. (Br.Don) AB23 — 15 E1
Scotstown Rd. (Br.Don) AB22 — 10 D6
Scotstown Rd. (Br.Don) AB23 — 10 D6
Scurdie Ness (Co.Bay) AB12 — 31 E5
Scylla Dr. (Co. Bay) AB12 — 37 E1
Scylla Gdns. (Co. Bay) AB12 — 37 E1
Scylla Gro. (Co. Bay) AB12 — 37 E1
Seafield Av. AB15 — 23 E4
Seafield Ct. AB15 — 23 E5
Seafield Cres. AB15 — 23 E5
Seafield Dr. E. AB15 — 23 E4
Seafield Dr. W. AB15 — 23 E5
Seafield Gdns. AB15 — 23 E5
Seafield Rd. AB15 — 23 E5
Seaforth Rd. AB24 — 15 E6

Seal Craig Gdns. AB12 — 30 D5
Seamount Ct. AB25 — 24 C1
  Gallowgate
Seamount Rd. AB25 — 5 D1
Seaton Av. AB24 — 15 E3
Seaton Cres. AB24 — 15 F3
Seaton Dr. AB24 — 15 E3
Seaton Gdns. AB24 — 15 E3
Seaton Ho. AB24 — 15 F3
Seaton Pl. AB24 — 15 E3
Seaton Pl. E. AB24 — 15 E3
Seaton Rd. AB24 — 15 E4
Seaton Wk. AB24 — 15 E3
Seaview Av. (Br.Don) AB23 — 11 E2
Seaview Circle (Br.Don) AB23 — 11 E3
Seaview Cl. (Br.Don) AB23 — 11 E2
Seaview Cres. (Br.Don) AB23 — 11 E3
Seaview Dr. (Br.Don) AB23 — 11 E3
Seaview Ho. AB24 — 15 F4
Seaview Pl. (Br.Don) AB23 — 11 E2
Seaview Rd. (Br.Don) AB23 — 15 E1
Seaview Ter. (Co.Bay) AB12 — 37 G1
Sedge Pl. (Port.) AB12 — 38 C4
Seurdie Ness AB12 — 31 E5
  Marchmont St.
Shapinsay Ct. AB15 — 22 A1
  Shapinsay Rd.
Shapinsay Rd. AB15 — 22 A1
Shapinsay Sq. AB15 — 22 A1
  Shapinsay Rd.
Shaw Circle, Westh. AB32 — 16 C4
Sheddocksley Dr. AB16 — 22 A1
Sheddocksley Rd. AB16 — 12 D6
Shepherd Pl. AB12 — 30 A2
Shetland Wk. AB16 — 12 C6
Shieldhill Gdns. AB12 — 31 E5
Shielhill Gdns. (Br.Don) AB22 — 10 C6
Shiprow AB11 — 5 D2
Shoe La. AB10 — 24 C1
  Queen St.
Shore Brae AB11 — 24 C2
  Shiprow
Shore La. AB11 — 24 D2
  Regent Quay
Short Loanings AB25 — 4 B1
Sillerton La. AB12 — 30 B2
Silverburn Cres. (Br.Don) AB23 — 11 E5
Silverburn Pl. (Br.Don) AB23 — 11 E5
Silverburn Rd. (Br.Don) AB22 — 10 C6
Simpson Rd. (Br.Don) AB23 — 15 E1
Sinclair Cres. (Co.Bay) AB12 — 30 D6
Sinclair Pl. AB11 — 25 E4
Sinclair Pl. (Co.Bay) AB12 — 31 E6
Sinclair Rd. AB11 — 24 D4
Sinclair Ter. (Co.Bay) AB12 — 31 E6
Skateraw Rd. (Newt.), Stone. AB39 — 41 E4
Skelly Rock AB12 — 31 E5
Skene La. AB25 — 4 B2
Skene Pl. AB10 — 24 A2
  Skene St.
Skene Pl. (Dyce) AB21 — 7 F3
Skene Rd. AB15 — 21 H2
Skene Sq. AB25 — 4 B1
Skene St. AB10 — 4 B2
Skene Ter. AB10 — 4 B2
Skye Rd. AB16 — 22 A1
Slains Av. (Br.Don) AB22 — 10 B5
Slains Circle (Br.Don) AB22 — 10 B5
Slains La. (Br.Don) AB22 — 10 C5
Slains Pl. (Br.Don) AB22 — 10 B6
Slains Rd. (Br.Don) AB22 — 10 B5
Slains St. (Br.Don) AB22 — 10 B5
Slains Ter. (Br.Don) AB22 — 10 B5
Slessor Dr. AB12 — 30 A4
Slessor Rd. AB12 — 30 A3
Sluie Dr. (Dyce) AB21 — 7 F2
Smithfield Ct. AB16 — 13 G3
Smithfield Dr. AB16 — 13 G3
Smithfield La. AB24 — 13 H3
Smithfield Rd. AB24 — 13 H3
Smithyhaugh Rd. AB16 — 12 D3
Society La. AB24 — 14 A3
Souter Circle, Westh. AB32 — 17 E4
Souter Gdns., Westh. AB32 — 17 E4
Souter Head Rd. AB12 — 30 D4
South Anderson Dr. AB10 — 23 G6
South Av. (Cults) AB15 — 28 A3
South Coll. St. AB11 — 5 D3

South Constitution St. AB24 — 24 D1
  Constitution St.
South Crown St. AB11 — 24 B4
South Deeside Rd. (Maryculter) — 28 C4
  AB12
South Esp. E. AB11 — 24 D4
South Esp. W. AB11 — 24 C4
South Grampian Circle AB11 — 24 D5
South Headlands Cres. (Newt.), — 41 E4
  Stone. AB39
South Mile End AB10 — 24 A5
South Mt. St. AB25 — 4 B1
South Silver St. AB10 — 24 B2
  Union St.
South Sq. AB11 — 25 F3
South Stocket La. AB16 — 13 F5
  Lilac Pl.
South Wk. AB16 — 13 H5
  Ash-hill Dr.
Southesk Pl. (Dyce) AB21 — 7 F2
Spa St. AB25 — 4 C1
Spademill La. AB15 — 23 F3
Spademill Rd. AB15 — 23 F3
Spark Ter. (Co.Bay) AB12 — 37 G1
Spey Rd. AB16 — 13 E6
Spey Ter. AB16 — 13 E6
Spital AB24 — 14 D5
Spital Wk. AB24 — 14 D5
Spring Gdn. AB25 — 5 C1
Spring Tyne, Westh. AB32 — 16 B4
Springbank Pl. AB11 — 24 B3
  Springbank St.
Springbank St. AB11 — 4 C3
Springbank Ter. AB11 — 4 C3
Springdale Ct. (Bield.) AB15 — 27 F3
Springdale Cres. (Bield.) AB15 — 27 F3
Springdale Pk. (Bield.) AB15 — 27 F3
Springdale Pl. (Bield.) AB15 — 27 F3
Springdale Rd. (Bield.) AB15 — 27 E3
Springfield Av. AB15 — 22 D4
Springfield Gdns. AB15 — 22 D5
Springfield La. AB15 — 22 D4
Springfield Pl. AB15 — 22 D5
Springfield Rd. AB15 — 23 E5
Springhill Cres. AB16 — 12 D5
Springhill Rd. AB16 — 12 D5
Springhill Ter. (Co.Bay) AB12 — 37 G1
  Spark Ter.
Springhill Ter. AB16 — 12 D5
Square, The (Port.) AB12 — 39 E3
Stafford St. AB25 — 14 C6
Stanley Ct., Westh. AB32 — 16 D5
  Parkside
Stanley St. AB10 — 4 A3
Station Brae, Peter. AB14 — 33 E3
Station Ms. (Bucks.) AB21 — 12 D1
  Oldmeldrum Rd.
Station Rd. (Cults) AB15 — 28 B2
Station Rd. (Bucks.) AB21 — 8 C6
Station Rd. (Dyce) AB21 — 7 F3
Station Rd. (Woodside) AB24 — 14 A2
Station Rd., Mill. AB13 — 26 B6
Station Rd. E., Mill. AB13 — 26 B6
Station Rd. E., Peter. AB14 — 33 E4
Station Rd. S., Peter. AB14 — 32 D4
Station Rd. W., Peter. AB14 — 32 D3
Stell Rd. AB11 — 5 D3
Stevenson Ct. AB25 — 24 A2
  Upper Denburn
Stevenson St. AB25 — 4 B2
Stewart Cres. AB16 — 13 E4
Stewart Pk. Ct. AB24 — 13 H4
Stewart Pk. Pl. AB24 — 13 H4
Stewart Ter. AB16 — 13 E4
Stirling St. AB11 — 24 C2
  Guild St.
Stocket Gra. AB16 — 13 G6
Stocket Par. AB16 — 13 F5
Stockethill Av. AB16 — 13 G6
  Stockethill Cres.
Stockethill Ct. AB16 — 13 G5
Stockethill Cres. AB16 — 13 G6
Stockethill La. AB16 — 13 G5
  Oldcroft Ter.
Stockethill Pl. AB16 — 13 G6
  Castleton Dr.
Stockethill Sq. AB16 — 13 G6
  Stockethill Cres.

Stockethill Way AB16	13	G5
Oldcroft Ter.		
Stonehaven Rd. AB12	38	B5
Stoneyhill Ter. AB12	37	G1
Stoneyton Ter. (Bucks.) AB21	8	B6
Stoneywood Pk. (Dyce) AB21	7	G6
Stoneywood Pk. N. (Dyce) AB21	7	G5
Stoneywood Rd. (Dyce) AB21	8	C5
Stoneywood Ter. (Bucks.) AB21	7	G6
Stornoway Cres. AB16	12	B6
Strachan Pl. AB16	13	F3
Fowler Av.		
Straik Pl., Westh. AB32	16	C5
Straik Rd., Westh. AB32	16	D5
Stranathro Ter. (Muchalls), Stone. AB39	40	C6
Strathbeg Pl. (Br.Don) AB22	14	D1
Davan Pk.		
Strathburn St. AB12	30	D5
Strathmore Dr. AB16	13	E5
Strawberry Bk. Par. AB11	4	B3
Stroma Ter. AB16	22	A1
Stronsay Av. AB15	22	C2
Stronsay Cres. AB15	22	C1
Stronsay Dr. AB15	22	C2
Stronsay Pl. AB15	22	C2
Sugarhouse La. AB11	24	D2
Mearns St.		
Sumburgh Cres. AB16	12	B6
Summer Pl. (Dyce) AB21	7	F3
Summer St. AB10	4	B2
Summer St. (Woodside) AB24	14	A3
Summerfield Pl. AB24	24	C1
Summerfield Ter.		
Summerfield Ter. AB24	5	D1
Summerhill Ct. AB15	22	D1
Summerhill Rd.		
Summerhill Cres. AB15	22	C1
Summerhill Dr. AB15	22	C1
Summerhill Rd. AB15	22	D1
Summerhill Ter. AB15	22	C2
Sunert Rd., Mill. AB13	26	D5
Sunnybank Pl. AB24	14	D5
Sunnybank Rd. AB24	14	D5
Sunnybrae (Bucks.) AB21	12	B2
Sunnyside Av. AB24	14	C5
Sunnyside Gdns. AB24	14	D5
Sunnyside Rd. AB24	14	C5
Sunnyside Ter. AB24	14	D5
Sunnyside Wk. AB24	14	D5
Sunnybank Pl.		
Swannay Rd. AB15	22	A1
Swannay Sq. AB15	22	A1
Shapinsay Rd.		
Sycamore Pl. AB11	24	B5
T		
Talisman Dr. AB10	29	E2
Talisman Rd. AB10	29	E2
Talisman Wk. AB10	29	E1
Tanfield Av. AB24	14	B3
Tanfield Ct. AB24	14	B3
Tanfield Wk.		
Tanfield Wk. AB24	14	B3
Taransay Ct. AB16	12	C6
Taransay Cres. AB16	12	C6
Taransay Rd. AB16	21	H1
Tarbothill Rd. AB22	14	C1
Tay Rd. AB16	13	E5
Tedder Rd. AB24	14	C3
Tedder St. AB24	14	C3
Tern Ct. (Newt.), Stone. AB39	41	E3
Tern Pl. AB23	11	E3
Tern Rd. (Co. Bay) AB12	30	D6
Teviot Rd. AB16	12	D6
Theatre La. AB11	24	D2
Regent Quay		
Thistle Ct. AB10	4	B2
Thistle Dr. (Port.) AB12	39	E2
Thistle La. AB10	4	B2
Thistle Pl. AB10	4	B3
Thistle Rd. (Dyce) AB21	6	C4
Thistle St. AB10	4	B3
Thomas Glover Pl. (Br.Don) AB22	14	D1
Thoms Ct. AB24	14	D4
High St.		
Thoms Pl. AB24	14	D4
High St.		
Thomson St. AB25	4	A1
Thomson St. La. AB25	23	H1
Loanhead Pl.		
Thorngrove Av. AB15	23	F5
Thorngrove Ct. AB15	23	F5
Thorngrove Cres. AB15	23	F5
Thorngrove Pl. AB15	23	F5
Tillydrone Av. AB24	14	D3
Tillydrone Ct. AB24	14	C2
Tillydrone Rd. AB24	14	C3
Tillydrone Ter. AB24	14	C3
Tiree Cres. AB16	22	A1
Todhead Gdns. AB12	31	E5
Todlaw Wk. (Dyce) AB21	7	G2
Tollohill Cres. AB12	30	C2
Tollohill Dr. AB12	30	C2
Tollohill Gdns. AB12	30	C2
Tollohill La. AB12	30	B2
Tollohill Pl. AB12	30	C2
Tollohill Sq. AB12	30	B2
Tornashean Gdns. (Dyce) AB21	7	G2
Towerview La., Peter. AB14	32	D2
Towerview Pk., Peter. AB14	32	D2
Towerview Rd., Peter. AB14	32	D2
Towerview Wk., Peter. AB14	32	D2
Towerview Way, Peter. AB14	32	D2
Towerview Wynd, Peter. AB14	32	D2
Towerview Rd.		
Trinity Ct., Westh. AB32	17	E4
Trinity La. AB11	24	C2
Exchange St.		
Trinity Quay AB11	5	D2
Trinity St. AB11	24	C2
Rennies Wynd		
Tulloch Pk. (Bucks.) AB21	12	B2
Newhills Av.		
Tullos Circle AB11	24	D5
Tullos Cres. AB11	25	E5
Tullos Pl. AB11	25	E5
Turnberry Ct. (Br.Don) AB22	10	C5
Turnberry Cres. (Br.Don) AB22	10	D5
Turnberry Gdns. (Br.Don) AB22	10	D5
Turnstone Ct. (Newt.), Stone. AB39	41	E3
Two Mile Cross AB10	29	G2
U		
Ugie Pl. AB16	13	E5
Uist Rd. AB16	21	H1
Union Br. AB11	24	B2
Union St.		
Union Glen AB11	4	B3
Union Glen Ct. AB11	24	A3
Union Glen		
Union Gro. AB10	4	A3
Union Gro. Ct. AB10	23	G4
Union Gro.		
Union Gro. La. AB10	23	H4
Union Row AB10	4	B3
Union Row (Dyce) AB21	7	F3
Union St. AB10	4	B3
Union St. AB11	4	B3
Union Ter. AB10	4	C2
Union Wynd AB10	4	B2
University Ct. (Bucks.) AB21	12	B2
University Rd. AB24	14	D4
Upper Denburn AB25	4	B2
Upper Fairburn Rd. AB21	7	E5
Upper Mastrick Way AB16	13	E5
Upperkirkgate AB10	5	D2
Urquhart La. AB24	15	E6
Urquhart Pl. AB24	15	F6
Urquhart Rd. AB24	15	E6
Urquhart St. AB24	15	F6
Urquhart Ter. AB24	15	F6
Usan Ness AB12	31	E5
V		
Valentine Cres. (Dane.) AB22	10	B6
Valentine Dr. (Dane.) AB22	10	A6
Valentine Rd. (Br.Don) AB22	10	A5
Valley Cres. AB12	30	C2
Valley Gdns. AB12	30	B2
Victoria Br. AB11	5	E3
Victoria Rd. AB11	24	D4
Victoria St. AB10	4	B2
Victoria St. (Dyce) AB21	7	F3
View Ter. AB25	4	A1
Viewfield Av. AB15	23	E5
Viewfield Cres. AB15	23	E5
Viewfield Gdns. AB15	22	D5
Viewfield Rd. AB15	22	D5
Viking Pl. (Port.) AB12	39	E2
Villagelands Rd. (Newt.), Stone. AB39	41	E4
Virginia Ct. AB11	24	C2
Justice St.		
Virginia St. AB11	5	D2
W		
Wagley Ct. (Bucks.) AB21	12	B2
Newhills Av.		
Wagley Par. (Bucks.) AB21	12	B2
Wagley Pl. (Bucks.) AB21	12	B2
Newhills Av.		
Wagrills La. AB24	14	D4
High St.		
Wales La. AB11	24	D2
Mearns St.		
Wales St. AB24	5	E1
Walker La. AB11	24	D4
Walker Pl. AB11	24	C4
Walker Rd. AB11	24	C5
Wallace Ho. AB15	22	B3
Hazlehead Rd.		
Wallacebrae Av. (Dane.) AB22	9	G6
Wallacebrae Cres. (Dane.) AB22	9	H6
Wallacebrae Dr. (Dane.) AB22	9	H6
Wallacebrae Gdns. (Br.Don) AB22	9	H6
Wallacebrae Path (Dane.) AB22	9	G6
Wallacebrae Ter.		
Wallacebrae Pl. (Dane.) AB22	9	H6
Wallacebrae Rd. (Dane.) AB22	9	H6
Wallacebrae Ter. (Dane.) AB22	9	G6
Wallacebrae Wk. (Dane.) AB22	9	G6
Wallacebrae Wynd (Dane.) AB22	9	H6
Wallfield Cres. AB25	4	A2
Wallfield Pl. AB25	4	A2
Walton Rd. (Bucks.) AB21	6	C3
Walton Rd. (Dyce) AB21	6	C6
Wapping St. AB11	5	C2
Wardhead Pl. AB16	12	C6
Watchman Brae (Bucks.) AB21	12	B3
Water La. AB11	24	D2
Mearns St.		
Waterloo Quay AB11	5	E2
Waterton Rd. (Bucks.) AB21	8	C5
Watson La. AB25	4	A1
Watson St. AB25	4	A1
Waulkmill Cres. AB16	13	E4
Waulkmill Rd. AB16	12	D4
Wavell Cres. AB24	14	B2
Waverley La. AB10	4	B2
Waverley Pl. AB10	4	B3
Weavers Row AB16	13	E4
Byron Cres.		
Webster Rd. AB12	30	A2
Weighhouse Sq. AB11	24	D2
Virginia St.		
Wellbrae Ter. AB15	23	E5
Wellgrove Cres., Westh. AB32	16	C5
Wellgrove Dr., Westh. AB32	16	C5
Wellgrove Rd.		
Wellgrove Rd., Westh. AB32	16	C5
Wellheads Cres. (Dyce) AB21	7	F5
Wellheads Dr. (Dyce) AB21	7	F5
Wellheads Ind. Est. (Dyce) AB21	7	F4
Wellheads Pl. (Dyce) AB21	7	F5
Wellheads Rd. (Dyce) AB21	7	G5
Wellheads Ter. (Dyce) AB21	7	F6
Wellheads Way (Dyce) AB21	7	F5
Wellington Brae AB11	24	C4
Wellington Br. AB11	24	C5
Wellington Circle (Altens) AB12	30	C4
Wellington Pl. AB11	5	C3
Wellington Rd. AB11	24	C5
Wellington Rd. AB12	30	B6
Wellington St. AB11	25	E2
Wellside Av. (Kings.) AB15	18	D3
Wellside Circle (Kings.) AB15	19	E3
Wellside Cl. (Kings.) AB15	19	E3
Wellside End (Kings.) AB15	19	E3
Wellside Gdns. (Kings.) AB15	18	D3
Wellside Pk. (Kings.) AB15	19	E3
Wellside Rd. (Kings.) AB15	19	E3
Wellside Wk. (Kings.) AB15	19	E3
Wellside Wynd (Kings.) AB15	19	E3

Wellwood Ter. (Cults) AB15	28	B2
West Cairncry Rd. AB16	13	F5
West Craibstone St. AB11	24	B3
Bon Accord Ter.		
West Cults Rd. (Cults) AB15	27	H4
West Mt. St. AB25	4	B1
West N. St. AB24	5	D1
West Tullos Ind. Est. AB12	30	C1
West Tullos Rd. AB12	30	C1
Westburn Ct. AB25	24	A1
Westburn Rd.		
Westburn Cres. AB25	14	A6
Westburn Dr. AB25	14	A5
Westburn Pk. AB25	14	B6
Westburn Rd. AB16	23	E1
Westburn Rd. AB25	4	A1
Westdyke Av., Westh. AB32	16	C5
Westdyke Cl., Westh. AB32	16	C4
Westdyke Ct., Westh. AB32	16	B5
Westdyke Dr., Westh. AB32	16	B5
Westdyke Gdns., Westh. AB32	16	B5
Westdyke Pl., Westh. AB32	16	C5
Westdyke Ter., Westh. AB32	16	B5
Westdyke Wk., Westh. AB32	16	C5
Westdyke Way, Westh. AB32	16	B5
Western Rd. AB24	14	B3
Westerton Cres. AB16	12	D3
Westerton Pl. (Cults) AB15	28	B3
Westerton Pl. AB16	13	F3
Marchburn Dr.		
Westerton Rd. (Cults) AB15	28	B3
Westfield Gdns., Westh. AB32	16	D4
Westfield Rd. AB25	4	A2
Westfield Ter. AB25	4	A2
Westgate (Bucks.) AB21	12	B2
Newhills Av.		
Westhill Business Pk., Westh. AB32	16	D5
Westhill Cres., Westh. AB32	16	D4
Westhill Dr., Westh. AB32	17	E4
Westhill Gra., Westh. AB32	16	C4
Westhill Hts., Westh. AB32	16	C3
Westhill Rd., Westh. AB32	17	F4
Westholme Av. AB15	22	D3
Westholme Cres. N. AB15	22	C3
Westholme Cres. S. AB15	22	C3
Westholme Ter. AB15	22	C3
Westray Cres. AB15	22	C1
Westray Rd. AB15	22	C1
Westwood Cres., Westh. AB32	16	D4
Westwood Dr., Westh. AB32	16	D4
Westwood Gro., Westh. AB32	16	D4
Westwood Pl., Westh. AB32	16	D4
Westwood Wk., Westh. AB32	16	D4
Westwood Way, Westh. AB32	16	D4
Whin Pk. Pl. AB16	13	E5
Whin Pk. Rd. AB16	13	E5
Whinhill Gdns. AB11	24	B5
Whinhill Gate AB11	24	B4
Whinhill Rd. AB11	24	A5
Whinpark Circle (Port.) AB12	38	D4
Whitehall Ms. AB25	23	H2
Whitehall Pl.		
Whitehall Pl. AB25	4	A2
Whitehall Rd. AB25	23	G2
Whitehall Ter. AB25	4	A2
Whitehills Cres. (Co.Bay) AB12	30	D6
Whitehills Ri. (Co.Bay) AB12	30	D6
Whitehills Way (Co.Bay) AB12	30	D6
Whitehouse St. AB10	4	B2
Whiteland Rd. (Newt.), Stone. AB39	41	E4
Murray Rd.		
Whitemyres Av. AB16	22	C1
Whitemyres Pl. AB16	22	C1
Whiterashes (Kings.) AB15	18	D6
Fairley Rd.		
Whitestripes Av. (Br.Don) AB22	10	A4
Whitestripes Cl. (Br.Don) AB22	10	B5
Whitestripes Cres. (Br.Don) AB22	10	B5
Whitestripes Dr. (Br.Don) AB22	10	A4
Whitestripes Path (Br.Don) AB22	10	B5
Whitestripes Pl. (Br.Don) AB22	10	B5
Whitestripes Rd. (Br.Don) AB22	9	H4
Whitestripes St. (Br.Don) AB22	10	B5
Whitestripes Way (Br.Don) AB22	10	B5
Wilkie Av. AB16	13	G3
Willow Wynd (Port.) AB12	38	C4
Willowbank Rd. AB11	24	A4
Willowdale Pl. AB24	5	D1
Willowgate Cl. AB11	24	A3
Hardgate		
Willowpark Cres. AB16	22	D1
Willowpark Pl. AB16	13	F6
Willowpark Rd. AB16	13	F6
Windford Rd. AB16	22	A1
Windford Sq. AB16	22	B1
Windmill Brae AB11	5	C2
Windmill La. AB11	24	B2
Windmill Brae		
Windsor Pl. AB10	24	A2
Victoria St.		
Windyedge Ct. (Newt.), Stone. AB39	40	D4
Wingate Pl. AB24	14	C3
Wingate Rd. AB24	14	C3
Wood St. AB11	25	F4
Wood St. La. AB11	25	F4
Woodburn Av. AB15	22	C4
Woodburn Cres. AB15	22	B4
Woodburn Gdns. AB15	22	C4
Woodburn Pl. AB15	22	C4
Woodcroft Av. (Br.Don) AB22	10	A2
Woodcroft Gdns. (Br.Don) AB22	10	A2
Woodcroft Gro. (Br.Don) AB22	10	A2
Woodcroft Rd. (Br.Don) AB22	10	A2
Woodcroft Wk. (Br.Don) AB22	10	A2
Woodcroft Av.		
Woodend Av. AB15	22	B2
Woodend Cres. AB15	22	B2
Woodend Dr. AB15	22	B2
Woodend Pl. AB15	22	B3
Woodend Rd. AB15	22	B2
Woodend Ter. AB15	22	C2
Woodhill Ct. AB16	13	G6
Castleton Dr.		
Woodhill Pl. AB15	23	E2
Woodhill Rd. AB15	23	E2
Woodhill Ter. AB15	23	E1
Woodlands Dr. AB21	6	C3
Woodlands Rd. AB21	6	C3
Woodside Rd. AB23	11	E4
Woodstock Rd. AB15	23	E2
Woolmanhill AB25	4	C2
Wright's & Cooper's Pl. AB24	14	D4
High St.		
Wrights Wk., Westh. AB32	17	E4
Wynford La., Westh. AB32	17	F4

Y

York Pl. AB11	25	E2
York St. AB11	25	E2
Ythan Rd. AB16	12	D6

Aberchirder 50 B2
Aberdeen 53 G3
Aberdeen Airport 53 F2
Aberlemno 54 D4
Aboyne 52 C4
Achath 53 E2
Affleck 53 F1
Aldie 51 F4
Aldivalloch 52 A1
Aldunie 52 A1
Alford 52 C2
Allancreich 52 C4
Allardice 55 G2
Altens 53 G3
Alyth 54 A5
Arbirlot 55 D5
Arbroath 55 E5
Arbuthnott 55 G2
Ardallie 51 F4
Ardgowse 52 D2
Ardiecow 50 A1
Ardlair 52 C1
Ardler 54 A5
Ardo 51 D4
Ardoyne 53 D1
Arnhall 55 E3
Arrat 55 E4
Arthrath 51 E4
Arthurstone 54 A5
Artrochie 51 F4
Ascreavie 54 B4
Asloun 52 C2
Aucharnie 50 B3
Auchattie 53 D4
Auchenblae 55 F2
Auchininna 50 B3
Auchintoul 52 C2
  Aberdeenshire
Auchintoul 50 B2
  Aberdeenshire
Auchiries 51 F4
Auchleven 52 D1
Auchlunies 53 F4
Auchmacoy 51 E4
Auchmair 52 A1
Auchmithie 55 E5
Auchmull 55 D2
Auchnacree 54 C3
Auchnagatt 51 E3
Aucholzie 52 A4
Auchorrie 53 D3
Auchronie 52 B5
Auchtertyre 54 A5
Auds 50 B1
Aulton 52 D1
Auquhorthies 53 F1

B
Backburn 50 A4
Backfolds 51 F2
Backhill 50 C4
Backhill of Clackriach 51 E3
Backhill of Trustach 52 D4
Badenscoth 50 B4
Badenyon 52 A2
Bainshole 50 B4
Balbithan 53 E2
Balchers 50 C2
Baldovie 54 B4
Balendoch 54 A4
Balfield 54 D3
Balfour 52 C4
Balgove 50 D4
Balgreen 50 C2
Balhalgardy 53 E1
Balhary 54 A5
Balkeerie 54 B5
Ballater 52 A4
Ballaterach 52 B4
Balloch 54 B4
Ballochan 52 C4
Ballogie 52 C4
Balmadies 54 D5
Balmedie 53 G2
Balnaboth 54 B3
Balnamoon 54 D3
Balthangie 50 D2
Bamff 54 A4
Banchory 53 E4
Banchory-Devenick 53 G3
Banff 50 B1
Bankhead 53 D2
  Aberdeenshire

Bankhead 53 D3
  Aberdeenshire
Bankhead Aberdeen 53 F3
Barnhead 55 E4
Barthol Chapel 50 D4
Baulds 52 D4
Bearnie 51 E4
Beggshill 50 A4
Belhelvie 53 G2
Belhinnie 52 B1
Bellabeg 52 A2
Bellaty 54 A4
Belliehill 55 D3
Benholm 55 G3
Benthoul 53 F3
Berryhillock 50 A1
Bieldside 53 F3
Birkenhills 50 C3
Birkhall 52 A4
Birse 52 C4
Birsemore 52 C4
Blackbraes 53 F2
Blackburn 53 F2
Blackchambers 53 E2
Blackdog 53 G2
Blackford 50 B4
Blackhill Aberdeenshire 51 F2
Blackhill Aberdeenshire 51 F3
Blackness 53 D4
Blacktop 53 F3
Blairshinnoch 50 B1
Blairydryne 53 E4
Blairythan Cottage 53 G1
Blindburn 51 E4
Boddam 51 G3
Bogbrae 51 F4
Bogfern 52 C3
Bogfields 52 C3
Bogfold 50 D2
Boghead 50 B2
Bogniebrae 50 A3
Bograxie 53 E2
Bogston 52 A3
Bogton 50 B2
Bolshan 55 E4
Bonnykelly 51 D2
Bonnyton 50 B4
  Aberdeenshire
Bonnyton Angus 55 E4
Borrowfield 53 F4
Boultenstone Hotel 52 B2
Boyndie 50 B1
Boysack 55 E5
Brackens 50 C2
Bracklach 52 A1
Bracklamore 50 D2
Bracobrae 50 A2
Braedownie 54 A2
Braefoot 50 C3
Braehead of Lunan 55 E4
Brathens 53 D4
Brechin 55 E3
Brideswell 50 A4
Bridge o' Ess 52 C4
Bridge of Alford 52 C2
Bridge of Bogendreip 53 D4
Bridge of Canny 53 D4
Bridge of Craigisla 54 A4
Bridge of Dee 53 D4
Bridge of Don 53 G3
Bridge of Dun 55 E4
Bridge of Dye 53 D5
Bridge of Feugh 53 D4
Bridge of Gairn 52 A4
Bridge of Muchalls 53 F4
Bridge of Muick 52 A4
Bridgend 50 A4
  Aberdeenshire
Bridgend Angus 54 D3
Bridgend of Lintrathen 54 A4
Bridgeton 52 C2
Broadsea 51 E1
Broomfield 51 E4
Broomhead 51 E1
Brownhill 51 D3
Bruntland 52 B1
Buchanhaven 51 G3
Bucksburn 53 F3
Bulwark 51 E3
Burn Farm 55 E2
Burnend 50 D3
Burnhaven 51 G3
Burnhervie 53 E2

Burnside Aberdeenshire 53 E2
Burnside Angus 54 D4

C
Cabrach 52 A1
Cairnbeathie 52 C3
Cairnbrogie 53 F1
Cairnbulg 51 F1
Cairness 51 F1
Cairnhill Aberdeenshire 53 G1
Cairnhill Aberdeenshire 50 B4
Cairnie 53 F3
Cairnorrie 51 D3
Caldhame 54 C5
Cambus o'May 52 B4
Cammachmore 53 G4
Candacraig 52 A4
Canterbury 50 A2
Carcary 55 E4
Cardno 51 E1
Careston 54 D3
Carmont 53 F5
Carmyllie 54 D5
Carnichal 51 E2
Carnousie 50 B2
Carrot 54 C5
Castleton 50 C2
  Aberdeenshire
Castleton Angus 54 B5
Catterline 55 G2
Cauldcots 55 E5
Causeyend 53 G2
Chapel Hill 51 F4
Chapel of Garioch 53 E1
Chapelton 53 F5
  Aberdeenshire
Chapelton Angus 55 E5
Charleston 54 B5
Charlestown 51 F1
  Aberdeenshire
Charlestown Aberdeen 53 G3
Clachnabrain 54 B3
Clatt 52 C1
Clatterin Brig 55 E2
Clinterty 53 F2
Clochtow 51 F4
Clockhill 51 D3
Clola 51 F3
Clova Aberdeenshire 52 B1
Clova Angus 54 B2
Clovenstone 53 E2
Cloverhill 53 G2
Clune Moray 50 A1
Clunie 50 B2
Cobairdy 50 A3
Coburty 51 E1
Coldwells 51 G3
Collieston 51 F5
Colliston 55 E5
Collmuir 52 C3
Collynie 50 D4
Colpy 50 B4
Comers 53 D3
Conland 50 B3
Cononsyth 55 D5
Contlaw 53 F3
Cookney 53 F4
Cookston 51 E4
Coralhill 51 F1
Cordach 52 D4
Cornhill 50 A2
Corrachree 52 B3
Corse 50 B3
Corse of Kinnoir 50 A3
Corsindae 53 D3
Cortachy 54 B4
Cothall 53 F3
Cottown Aberdeenshire 52 C1
Cottown Aberdeenshire 50 D4
Cottown Aberdeenshire 53 E2
Coull 52 C3
Coupar Angus 54 A5
Cove Bay 53 G3
Cowie 53 F5
Coynach 52 B3
Craibstone 53 F2
Craichie 54 C5
Craigculter 51 E2
Craigdam 50 D4
Craigearn 53 E2
Craigellie 51 F1
Craigie 53 G2
Craigie Brae 51 D4

Craiglug 53 F4
Craigmaud 51 D2
Craigmyle House 52 D3
Craigo 55 E3
Craigton Aberdeen 53 F3
Craigton Angus 54 B4
Craik 52 B1
Cranna 50 B2
Craskins 52 C3
Crathes 53 E4
Crawton 55 G2
Crichie 51 E3
Crimond 51 F2
Crimonmogate 51 F2
Crofts of Haddo 50 D4
Crombie Mill 54 D5
Cromblet 50 C4
Cross of Jackson 50 C4
Crossroads 53 E4
Crovie 50 D1
Cruchie 50 A3
Cruden Bay 51 F4
Culdrain 50 A4
Cullen 50 A1
Culsh 52 A4
Cultercullen 53 G1
Cults Aberdeenshire 50 A4
Cults Aberdeen 53 F3
Culvie 50 A2
Cuminestown 50 D2
Cushnie 50 C1
Cuttyhill 51 F2

D
Dalbog 55 D2
Dalfad 52 A3
Dalmadilly 53 E2
Danestone 53 G2
Darnabo 50 C3
Darnford 53 E4
Darra 50 C3
Dartfield 51 F2
Davan 52 B3
Daviot 53 E1
Deecastle 52 B4
Delfrigs 53 G1
Delphorrie 52 B2
Denend 50 A4
Denhead Aberdeenshire 53 E2
Denhead Aberdeenshire 51 E2
Denhead of Arbirlot 55 E5
Denmill 53 F2
Denmoss 50 B3
Denside 53 F4
Dinnet 52 B4
Dorsell 52 C2
Douglastown 54 C5
Dounepark 50 C1
Douneside 52 B3
Downies 53 G4
Drumblade 50 A3
Drumblair 50 B3
Drumgley 54 C5
Drumhead 52 D4
Drumlasie 52 D3
Drumlithie 53 E5
Drumnagorrach 50 A2
Drumoak 53 E4
Drums 53 G1
Drumwhindle 51 E4
Drunkendub 55 E5
Drymuir 51 E3
Dubford 50 C1
Dubton 55 D4
Dulax 52 A2
Dun 55 E4
Duncanston 52 C1
Dunecht 53 E3
Dunlappie 55 D3
Dunnichen 54 D5
Durno 53 E1
Dyce 53 F2
Dykehead 54 B3
Dykelands 55 F3
Dykends 54 A4
Dykeside 50 C3

E
Earlsford 50 D4
Eassie and Nevay 54 B5
East Auchronie 53 F3
East Cairnbeg 55 F2
East Davoch 52 B3

East Learney 52 D3
East Mains 53 D4
Easter Knox 55 D5
Easter Lednathie 54 B3
Easter Ord 53 F3
Easter Tulloch 55 F2
Easter Whyntie 50 B1
Ecclesgreig 55 F3
Echt 53 E3
Edinbanchory 52 B2
Edzell 55 D3
Ellon 51 E4
Elrick *Aberdeenshire* 53 F3
Elrick *Moray* 52 B1
Errollston 51 F4
Esslemont 53 G1
Ethie Mains 55 E5

F
Fairley 53 F3
Farmtown 50 A2
Farnell 55 E4
Fattahead 50 B2
Fawsyde 55 G2
Feith-hill 50 B3
Fern 54 C3
Fernybank 54 D2
Ferryden 55 F4
Fetterangus 51 E2
Fettercairn 55 E2
Fetternear House 53 E2
Feus of Caldhame 55 E3
Fichlie 52 B2
Finavon 54 C4
Findon 53 G4
Fingask 53 E1
Finnygaud 50 B2
Fintry 50 C2
Finzean 52 C4
Fisherford 50 B4
Fishtown of Usan 55 F4
Fleuchats 52 A3
Flushing 51 F3
Folla Rule 50 C4
Forbestown 52 A2
Fordoun 55 F2
Fordyce 50 A1
Forfar 54 C4
Fortrie 50 B3
Foulzie 50 C1
Foveran House 53 G1
Fraserburgh 51 E1
Frendraught 50 B3
Friockheim 55 D5
Fyvie 50 C4

G
Gallery 55 E3
Gallowfauld 54 C5
Gamrie 50 C1
Gannochy 55 E2
Gardenstown 50 C1
Garlogie 53 E3
Garmond 50 D2
Gartly 50 A4
Garvock 55 F2
Gask *Aberdeenshire* 51 F3
Gask *Aberdeenshire* 50 C3
Gateside 52 D2
  Aberdeenshire
Gateside *Angus* 54 C5
Glamis 54 B5
Glanderston 52 C1
Glascorrie 52 A4
Glashmore 53 E3
Glassel 53 D4
Glasterlaw 55 D4
Glenarm 54 B3
Glenbervie 53 E5
Glencat 52 C4
Glencuie 52 B2
Glendoll Lodge 54 A2
Glendye Lodge 52 D5
Glenhead Farm 54 A3
Glenkindie 52 B2
Glenlee 52 B5
Glenmoy 54 C3
Glenogil 54 C3
Glenprosen Village 54 B3
Glenquiech 54 C3
Glensaugh 55 E2
Glenshalg 52 C3
Glenton 52 D1

Gordonstown 50 A2
  Aberdeenshire
Gordonstown 50 C4
  Aberdeenshire
Gorrachie 50 C2
Gourdas 50 C3
Gourdon 55 G2
Gowanhill 51 F1
Grainhow 51 D3
Grantlodge 53 E2
Greendams 52 D4
Greenhall 52 D1
Greenheads 51 F4
Greenlaw 50 B2
Greenmyre 50 D4
Greystone 54 D5
Guthrie 55 D4
Guynd 55 D5

H
Hardgate 53 E3
Hatton 51 F4
Hatton Castle 50 C3
Hatton of Fintray 53 F2
Hattoncrook 53 F1
Haughs 50 A3
Hayhillock 54 D5
Hazelhead 53 F3
Heathcot 53 F3
Heugh-head 52 A2
  Aberdeenshire
Heugh-head 52 C4
  Aberdeenshire
Hillbrae *Aberdeenshire* 50 B3
Hillbrae *Aberdeenshire* 53 E1
Hillbrae *Aberdeenshire* 50 D4
Hillhead of Auchentumb 51 E2
Hillhead of Cocklaw 51 F3
Hillockhead 52 A3
  Aberdeenshire
Hillockhead 52 B2
  Aberdeenshire
Hillside *Aberdeenshire* 53 G4
Hillside *Angus* 55 F3
Hilton Croft 51 E4
Hirn 53 E3
Hoggie 50 A1
Horniehaugh 54 C3
Howe of Teuchar 50 C3
Huntly 50 A3
Hythie 51 F2

I
Idvies 54 D5
Inch of Arnhall 55 E2
Inchbare 55 E3
Inchbraoch 55 F4
Inchgrundle 54 C2
Inchmarlo 53 D4
Inchnabobart 52 A5
Inchock 55 E5
Inkhorn 51 E4
Insch 52 D1
Inverallochy 51 F1
Inverarity 54 C5
Inverbervie 55 G2
Inverebrie 51 E4
Inverkeilor 55 E5
Inverkeithny 50 B3
Invernettie 51 G3
Inverquharity 54 C4
Inverquhomery 51 F3
Inverugie 51 G3
Inverurie 53 E1
Invery House 53 D4
Inverythan 50 C3
Ironside 51 D2

J
Jackstown 50 C4
Johnshaven 55 F3
Johnston Mains 55 F3
Jordanstone 54 A5

K
Kebholes 50 B2
Keig 52 D2
Keilhill 52 C2
Keillor 54 A5
Keithock 55 E3
Kemnay 53 E2
Kennerty 53 D4
Kennethmont 52 C1

Kildrummy 52 B2
Kinblethmont 55 E5
Kincaldrum 54 C5
Kincardine O'Neil 52 C4
Kincorth 53 G3
Kincraig 53 G1
Kinellar 53 F2
Kingsford 50 C3
  Aberdeenshire
Kingsford 52 C2
  Aberdeenshire
Kingsford *Aberdeen* 53 F3
Kingsmuir 54 C5
Kingswells 53 F3
Kinharrachie 51 E4
Kinknockie 51 F3
Kinloch 54 A5
Kinmuck 53 F2
Kinnadie 51 E3
Kinneff 55 G2
Kinnell 55 E4
Kinnettles 54 C5
Kinnordy 54 B4
Kintocher 52 C3
Kintore 53 E2
Kiplaw Croft 51 F4
Kirkbuddo 54 D5
Kirkhill 55 E3
Kirkinch 54 B5
Kirkney 50 A4
Kirkstile 50 A4
Kirkton *Aberdeenshire* 52 D1
Kirkton *Aberdeenshire* 50 B2
Kirkton *Aberdeenshire* 52 D2
Kirkton *Angus* 54 C5
Kirkton of Airlie 54 B4
Kirkton of Bourtie 53 F1
Kirkton of Craig 55 F4
Kirkton of Culsalmond 50 B4
Kirkton of Durris 53 E4
Kirkton of Glenbuchat 52 A2
Kirkton of Glenisla 54 A3
Kirkton of Kingoldrum 54 B4
Kirkton of Logie Buchan 53 F1
Kirkton of Maryculter 53 F4
Kirkton of Menmuir 54 D3
Kirkton of Rayne 50 B4
Kirkton of Skene 53 F3
Kirktonhill 55 E3
Kirktown 51 F2
Kirktown of Alvah 51 F2
Kirktown of Auchterless 50 C3
Kirktown of Deskford 50 A1
Kirktown of Fetteresso 53 F5
Kirktown of Slains 51 F5
Kirriemuir 54 B4
Knabbygates 50 A2
Knaven 51 D3
Knock 50 A2
Knowes of Elrick 50 B2
Knowehead 51 E2

L
Ladysford 51 E1
Laithers 50 B3
Landerberry 53 E3
Largie 50 B4
Largue 50 B3
Lary 52 A3
Lauchintilly 53 E2
Laurencekirk 55 F2
Leask 51 F4
Leitfie 54 A5
Lemnas 50 D1
Leochel-Cushnie 52 C2
Leschangie 53 E2
Leslie 52 C1
Lessendrum 50 A3
Letham 54 D5
Lethenty 50 D3
Ley 52 C2
Leylodge 53 E2
Leys *Aberdeenshire* 51 F2
Leys *Aberdeenshire* 52 B3
Leys of Cossans 54 B5
Leysmill 55 E5
Limehillock 50 A2
Lindertis 54 B4
Linhead 50 B2
Linn of Muick Cottage 52 B5
Lintmill 50 A1
Little Brechin 55 D3
Little Dens 51 F3

Little Idoch 50 C3
Little Ley 52 D2
Loanhead 51 E4
Lochlair 54 D5
Lochside 55 F3
Logie *Angus* 55 E3
Logie *Angus* 54 B4
Logie Coldstone 52 B3
Logie Newton 50 B4
Logie Pert 55 E3
Longdrum 53 G2
Longhill 51 E2
Longlands 52 B1
Longmanhill 50 C1
Longside 51 F3
Lour 54 C5
Lownie Moor 54 C5
Lumphanan 52 C3
Lumsden 52 B1
Lunan 55 E4
Lunanhead 54 C4
Lunderton 51 G3
Luthermuir 55 E3
Lyne 53 E3
Lyne of Skene 53 E2

M
Macduff 50 C1
Macterry 50 C3
Mains of Balgavies 54 D4
Mains of Balhall 54 D3
Mains of Ballindarg 54 C4
Mains of Culsh 51 D3
Mains of Dillavaird 53 E5
Mains of Drum 53 F3
Mains of Dudwick 51 E4
Mains of Fedderate 51 D3
Mains of Glack 53 E1
Mains of Glassaugh 50 A1
Mains of Glenbuchat 52 A2
Mains of Linton 53 E3
Mains of Melgund 54 D4
Mains of Pitfour 51 E3
Mains of Pittrichie 53 F1
Mains of Thornton 55 E2
Mannofield 53 G3
Marcus 54 D4
Marnoch 50 A2
Maryhill 50 D3
Marykirk 55 E3
Maryton 55 E4
Marywell 53 G4
  Aberdeenshire
Marywell 52 C4
  Aberdeenshire
Marywell *Angus* 55 E5
Mastrick 53 F3
Maud 51 E3
Mayen 50 A3
Meigle 54 A5
Meikle Strath 55 E2
Meikle Tarty 53 G1
Meikle Wartle 50 C4
Melgum 52 B3
Melrose 50 C1
Memsie 51 E1
Memus 54 C4
Menie House 53 G1
Mergie 53 E5
Methlick 51 D4
Mid Ardlaw 51 E1
Mid Beltie 52 D3
Mid Cairncross 54 D2
Middle Drums 55 D4
Middlehill 50 D3
Middleton 53 F2
  Aberdeenshire
Middleton *Angus* 55 D5
Middleton of Potterton 53 G2
Middleton Park 53 G2
Midtown of Barras 53 F5
Migvie 52 B3
Milbethill 50 B2
Mill of Colp 50 C3
Mill of Elrick 51 E3
Mill of Kingoodie 53 F1
Mill of Monquich 53 F4
Mill of Uras 55 G2
Millbank 51 F3
Millbreck 51 F3
Millburn *Aberdeenshire* 52 C1
Millburn *Aberdeenshire* 50 B4
Millden 53 G2

Name		
Milldens	54	D4
Milltimber	53	F3
Milltown	52	B2
Milltown of Craigston	50	C2
Milltown of Rothiemay	50	A3
Milltown of Towie	52	B2
Milton *Angus*	54	B5
Milton *Moray*	50	A1
Milton of Auchinhove	52	C3
Milton of Campfield	52	D3
Milton of Coldwells	51	E4
Milton of Cullerlie	53	E3
Milton of Cushnie	52	C2
Milton of Inveramsay	53	E1
Milton of Noth	52	C1
Milton of Tullich	52	A4
Minnes	53	G1
Minnonie	50	C1
Mintlaw	51	F3
Monkshill	50	C3
Monteach	51	D3
Montgarrie	52	C2
Montrose	55	F4
Monymusk	53	D2
Morphie	55	F3
Moss-side	50	A2
Mossat	52	B2
Mosshead	50	A4
Mosside of Ballinshoe	54	C4
Mosston	54	D5
Mounie Castle	53	E1
Mountblairy	50	B2
Mowtie	53	F5
Muchalls	53	F4
Muckletown	52	C1
Muir of Fowlis	52	C2
Muirden	50	C2
Muirhead	52	C2
Muirtack *Aberdeenshire*	51	E4
Muirtack *Aberdeenshire*	50	D3
Muirton of Ballochy	55	E3
Muiryfold	50	C2
Mundurno	53	G2
Murthill	54	C4
Myrebird	53	E4

N

Name		
Nether Crimond	53	F1
Nether Glasslaw	51	D2
Nether Handwick	54	B5
Nether Kinmundy	51	F3
Nether Lenshie	50	B3
Nether Pitforthie	55	G2
Netherbrae	50	C2
Netherley	53	F4
Nethermuir	51	E3
Netherton	54	D4
New Aberdour	51	D1
New Alyth	54	A5
New Byth	50	D2
New Deer	51	D3
New Leeds	51	E2
New Leslie	52	C1
New Mains of Ury	53	F5
New Pitsligo	51	D2
Newbigging *Aberdeenshire*	53	F4
Newbigging *Angus*	54	A5
Newburgh *Aberdeenshire*	51	E2
Newburgh *Aberdeenshire*	53	G1
Newmachar	53	F2
Newmill *Aberdeenshire*	53	E5
Newmill *Aberdeenshire*	51	D3
Newmill *Aberdeenshire*	53	F1
Newmill of Inshewan	54	C3
Newnoth	50	A4
Newseat	50	C4
Newton	51	F3
Newtonhill	53	G4
Newtonmill	55	E3
Newtyle	54	A5
Nigg	53	G3
Noranside	54	C3
North Essie	51	F2
North Millbrex	50	D3
North Tarbothill	53	G2
Northburnhill	50	D3
Northfield *Aberdeenshire*	50	D1

Name		
Northfield *Aberdeen*	53	F3
Northmuir	54	B4

O

Name		
Oathlaw	54	C4
Ogil	54	C3
Old Aberdeen	53	G3
Old Craig	53	G1
Old Crombie	50	A2
Old Deer	51	E3
Old Kinnernie	53	E3
Old Leslie	52	C1
Old Rattray	51	F2
Old Rayne	53	D1
Oldhall	52	B4
Oldmeldrum	53	F1
Oldmill	52	C3
Oldtown of Ord	50	B2
Oldwhat	51	D2
Ordhead	53	D2
Ordie	52	B3
Orrok House	53	G2
Overbrae	50	D2
Overton *Aberdeenshire*	53	E2
Overton *Aberdeen*	53	F2
Oyne	53	D1

P

Name		
Padanaram	54	C4
Park	50	A2
Parkford	54	C4
Parkhill	55	E5
Parkneuk	55	F2
Pathhead	55	F3
Pearsie	54	B4
Peathill	51	E1
Pennan	50	D1
Percie	52	C4
Perkhill	52	C3
Pert	55	E3
Peterculter	53	F3
Peterhead	51	G3
Petty	50	C4
Pettymuick	53	G1
Phesdo	55	E2
Pitblae	51	E1
Pitcaple	53	E1
Pitfichie	53	D2
Pitinnan	50	C4
Pitkennedy	54	D4
Pitmedden	53	F1
Pitmuies	55	D5
Pitmunie	53	D2
Pittodrie House	53	D1
Plaidy	50	C2
Port Elphinstone	53	E2
Port Errol	51	F4
Portlethen	53	G4
Portlethen Village	53	G4
Portsoy	50	A1
Potarch	52	D4
Potterton	53	G2
Protstonhill	50	D1

Q

Name		
Quilquox	51	E4

R

Name		
Raemoir House	53	D4
Rathen	51	F1
Raxton	51	D4
Redcastle	55	E4
Redcloak	53	F5
Redford *Aberdeenshire*	55	F3
Redford *Angus*	55	D5
Redheugh	54	C3
Redhill *Aberdeenshire*	50	B4
Redhill *Aberdeenshire*	53	E3
Redhill *Moray*	50	A3
Redhouse	52	C1
Rescobie	54	D4
Reswallie	54	D4
Rhynie	52	B1
Rickarton	53	F5
Rinmore	52	B2
Roadside of Kinneff	55	G2
Rora	51	F2
Rorandle	53	D2
Rosehearty	51	E1
Rosehill	52	C4
Rossie Farm School	55	E4
Rothiebrisbane	50	C4
Rothienorman	50	C4

Name		
Rottal	54	B3
Runtaleave	54	A3
Ruthrieston	53	G3
Ruthven *Aberdeenshire*	50	A3
Ruthven *Angus*	54	A5

S

Name		
Saint Combs	51	F1
Saint Cyrus	55	F3
Saint Fergus	51	G2
Saint Katherines	50	C4
Saint Vigeans	55	E5
Sandend	50	A1
Sandfordhill	51	G3
Sandhaven	51	E1
Sauchen	53	D2
Sauchieburn	55	E3
Scotston	55	F3
Seatown *Aberdeenshire*	51	G2
Seatown *Moray*	50	A1
Shanzie	54	A4
Shielhill	54	C4
Shiels	53	D3
Sillyearn	50	A2
Silvermoss	50	D4
Sinnahard	52	B2
Skares	50	B4
Skelmonae	51	D4
Skelmuir	51	E3
Slack	50	A4
Slains Park	55	G2
Slioch	50	A4
Smallburn	51	F3
South Blackbog	50	C4
South Flobbets	50	C4
South Kirkton	53	E3
South Redbriggs	50	C3
South Upper Barrack	51	E3
Southend	50	C3
Southmuir	54	B4
Spittal of Glenmuick	52	A5
Springleys	50	C4
Steinmanhill	50	C3
Stirling	51	G3
Stonehaven	53	F5
Stoneywood	53	F2
Stracathro	55	E3
Strachan	53	D4
Straloch	53	F1
Strathdon	52	A2
Strathgirnock	52	A4
Strichen	51	E2
Stuartfield	51	E3
Sunnyside	53	F4

T

Name		
Tanglandford	51	D4
Tannachie	53	E5
Tannadice	54	C4
Tarfside	52	B5
Tarland	52	B3
Tarves	51	D4
Tavelty	53	E2
Tayock	55	E4
Templewood	55	E3
Tepersie Castle	52	C1
Teuchan	51	F4
Tewel	53	F5
Thainston	55	E2
Thainstone House	53	E2
The Banking	50	C4
The Birks	53	E3
The Burn	55	D2
The Drums	54	B3
The Neuk	54	E4
Thomastown	50	A4
Thornton	54	B5
Thornyhill	55	E2
Thunderton	51	F3
Tifty	50	C3
Tigerton	54	D3
Tillery	53	G1
Tillyarblet	54	D3
Tillybirloch	53	D3
Tillycairn Castle	53	D2
Tillycorthie	53	G1
Tillydrine	52	D4
Tillyfar	51	D3
Tillyfour	52	C2
Tillyfourie	52	D2
Tillygreig	53	F1
Tillypronie	52	B3
Tipperty *Aberdeenshire*	53	E5

Name		
Tipperty *Aberdeenshire*	53	G1
Tocher	50	B4
Todlachie	53	D2
Toll of Birness	51	F4
Torbeg	52	A3
Tornaveen	52	D3
Torphins	52	D3
Torrancroy	52	A2
Torry	53	G3
Torterston	51	F3
Toux	51	E2
Towie *Aberdeenshire*	51	D1
Towie *Aberdeenshire*	52	C1
Towie *Aberdeenshire*	52	B2
Trinity	55	E3
Tulloch	50	D4
Tullochvenus	52	C3
Tullos	54	D5
Tullyfergus	54	A5
Tullynessle	52	C2
Turclossie	51	D2
Turin	54	D4
Turriff	50	C2

U

Name		
Udny Green	53	F1
Udny Station	53	G1
Union Croft	53	F4
Upper Boyndlie	51	E1
Upper Burnhaugh	53	F4
Upper Hawkhillock	51	F4
Upper Lochton	53	D4
Upper Muirskie	53	F4
Upper Ridinghill	51	F2

W

Name		
Wardhouse	50	A4
Wartle	52	C3
Waterhill of Bruxie	51	E3
Waterloo	51	F4
Waterside *Aberdeenshire*	52	A2
Waterside *Aberdeenshire*	51	F5
Weachyburn	50	B2
Wedderlairs	51	D4
West Cairncake	50	D3
West Muir	55	D3
West Park	53	E4
Wester Badentyre	50	C2
Wester Culbeuchly	50	B1
Wester Fintray	53	F2
Wester Foffarty	54	C5
Wester Greenskares	50	C1
Wester Ord	53	F3
Westerton *Aberdeenshire*	53	E4
Westerton *Angus*	55	E4
Westhall	53	D1
Westhill	53	F3
Westmuir	54	B4
Westside	53	F4
Wheedlemont	52	B1
Wheen	54	B2
Whigstreet	54	C5
Whinnyfold	51	F4
Whitebog	51	E2
Whitecairns	53	G2
Whitefield	53	E1
Whiteford	53	E1
Whitehills	50	B1
Whitehouse	52	D2
Whiterashes	53	F1
Whitestone	52	D4
Whitestripe	51	E2
Whitewell	51	E1
Whitlam	53	F1
Witton	55	D3
Woodend	53	D2
Woodhead	50	C4
Woodside	53	G3
Wrae	50	C2
Wrangham	50	B4

Y

Name		
Yonder Bognie	50	A3
Ythanwells	50	B4
Ythsie	51	D4